FOOLPROOF

FISH

60 DELICIOUS DISHES TO MAKE AT HOME

LIBBY SILBERMANN

PHOTOGRAPHY BY
RITA PLATTS

Hardie Grant

QUADRILLE

Publishing Director
Sarah Lavelle

Editor
Stacey Cleworth

Series Designer
Emily Lapworth

Designer
Alicia House

Photographer
Rita Platts

Food Stylist
Libby Silbermann

Prop Stylist
Louie Waller

Head of Production
Stephen Lang

Production Controller
Sabeena Atchia

First published in 2022 by Quadrille,
an imprint of Hardie Grant Publishing

Quadrille
52–54 Southwark Street
London SE1 1UN
quadrille.com

Text © Quadrille 2022
Photography © Rita Platts 2022
Design and layout © Quadrille 2022

Cataloguing in Publication Data: a catalogue
record for this book is available from the
British Library.

9781787137912

Printed in China

FSC
www.fsc.org

MIX
Paper from
responsible sources
FSC™ C020056

CONTENTS

INTRODUCTION

This book contains 60 foolproof recipes for cooking fish and seafood. It is designed to take the stress out of cooking fish and provide you with easy, delicious recipes to go back to time and time again. Buying and eating fish have rightly come under more scrutiny in recent years, but with some sensible choices you can consume fish in the same way as many do meat: see it as a treat rather than something to be eaten every single day, and try to buy from sustainable sources.

Many people are daunted by the prospect of cooking fish or seafood. Will I overcook it? How do I fillet it? Shellfish at home – won't I poison everyone?! However, there is no need to worry as fish and seafood are simple to prepare and incredibly versatile. Fish is a great option when cooking for friends, whether it's something that little bit special or a nutritious and easy midweek meal.

This book is divided into three chapters. Brunch & Light Bites contains recipes for a late breakfast, a lighter lunch or for snacks, and includes dishes such as speedy mackerel pâté, tuna poke bowls and pork and prawn

gyoza. My Quick & Easy recipes are exactly as described, meaning they are ideal for lunches and midweek dinners – you'll find recipes such as yellow prawn laksa soup, curry-spiced kedgeree and easy herby cod goujons. The final chapter, Something Special, is packed full of recipes which either take a little longer to make or use particularly special ingredients. Recipes such as my ultimate fish tacos, seafood orzo paella and spaghetti vongole create beautiful centrepieces for elegant starters, memorable dinners for two or feasts for a crowd.

I hope you enjoy cooking from this book as much as I enjoyed devising it; fish and seafood are delicacies that should be treated with respect and are worth celebrating.

Happy cooking!

Libby

SUSTAINABILITY & SEASONALITY

It can seem daunting to buy and shop for fish sustainably when there are warnings about overfishing in UK waters and overseas. But, like everything, moderation is key. Shopping for, preparing and eating fish should be a treat, and with the recipes in this book you can do so in the best possible way.

Where to buy from

If possible, try to buy from a fishmonger or the fish counter at your local supermarket – these places are the most likely to supply fish and seafood that is farmed in a sustainable way. Ask the fishmonger where the fish has come from, what fish is best to buy in the current season and what they recommend in general. This way you are less likely to buy pre-frozen produce that has been mass-fished overseas.

Resources

To help ensure you make the best decisions when trying to buy fish from sustainable sources, here are some helpful websites with information.

UK: mcsuk.org and msc.org

USA: seafoodwatch.org and sustainablefish.org

Canada: seachoice.org and livingoceans.org

Australia: goodfish.org.au and marineconservation.org.au/ sustainable-seafood-choices

New Zealand: www.seafood.org.nz

Seasonality

It is always best to consider the seasons when choosing all your ingredients, not only fish. If you are buying produce in line with the seasons, not only will you be doing your bit to support sustainability, but you will benefit from the best taste, too. Here is a list of which seasonally available fish and seafood in the UK.

Spring (March, April, May): plaice, mackerel, sprats, haddock, lobster, scallops, oysters, mussels, crab, squid

Summer (June, July, August): sea bass, pollock, turbot, mullet, bream, plaice, hake, monkfish, langoustines

Autumn (September, October, November): cod, skate, red mullet

Winter (December, January, February): sardines, brill, cuttlefish, clams

BUYING & FREEZING TIPS

When buying and choosing whole fish, there are a few tips and signs you should be aware of to make sure the fish is fresh and safe to eat.

• Fish should smell salty, like the sea, but should not have an overpowering or unpleasant 'fish' smell.

• The eyes on a whole fish should be clear and bright – they should stick out of the head of the fish instead of being sunken or too cloudy.

• There should be a natural slime or wetness to the fish skin – it shouldn't be dry or flaky.

• The scales on the fish should be shiny and intact – avoid the fish if it has lots of broken scales or patches missing.

• The gills (located by the head) of a fish should be bright pink or red, not greyish or brown.

It is sometimes trickier to gauge freshness when buying fillets of fish but some of the same rules apply: make sure the flesh feels firm to the touch, rather than soft. The fillets should smell of the sea but not of have an unpleasant fish smell, and there should be no discoloration of the flesh.

It is always best to buy fish fresh and therefore eat it fresh – the day you buy it. It will taste its very best and avoids

any chance of bacteria developing. However, if you do need to store it in the fridge, wrap it well in clingfilm (plastic wrap) and consume within 2 days (depending on best before date). Fish can be frozen; however, it will deteriorate after time. Try not to freeze fish raw fish for longer than three to eight months.

Freezing seafood is not advisable, though you can freeze raw prawns or scallops more easily as these are not live. Freezing mussels, clams, crab etc requires freezing them in their shell and when they are live.

Sushi-grade tuna

Sushi-grade tuna is actually a fairly misleading title or grade system. In its simplest terms it means fish that the seller has deemed suitable for raw consumption; however, there is no official or FDA-approved grading system. It is always best to approach a fishmonger and speak to them about which fish they deem safe for raw consumption – most often this is what's labelled as 'sushi-grade' for consumers and shoppers.

FISH PREPARATION

Preparing a whole fish can appear difficult at first, but with these simple and efficient steps it shouldn't be. If you are buying from a fishmonger or fish counter, you can always ask them to prepare the fish this way too.

Descaling the fish is simply scrubbing away the tough, looser scales on the outside skin. There is nothing too technical needed here apart from a little elbow grease. There are specific descaling tools you can buy, but a good kitchen knife is sufficient. Using the blunt edge of the knife, simply hold the fish by its head and then scrape and drag the knife against the grain of the scales towards you to remove them. Then turn the fish over and repeat on the other side. It's always easiest to do this in the sink so you can wash away the excess scales. After the fish is descaled, run your fingers along the skin – it should feel smooth.

Gutting a fish is usually a job for your fishmonger, but if you do fancy buying or catching one and trying for yourself, then this is the simplest method to follow. Press your palm on to the body of the fish and then use a knife to cut up the belly towards the head. Pull out all the guts and entrails from inside, washing the fish under the tap to remove any blood. You should be left with just the bones, carcass and fillets. Gutting is also essential if you wish to fillet the fish, and it should be done as soon as possible if you have caught your own.

Filleting a fish is surprisingly simple, but again if you are worried about ruining your fish, it is best to ask your fishmonger to do this for you. Start by holding the fish by its head and pulling back, or cutting off with scissors, the small fin by its head. Then make a cut at a 45-degree angle behind the head until you reach the backbone. Run a small, sharp knife along the backbone, cutting the flesh away from the bone, trying to keep as close to the bone as possible to avoid losing any of the flesh. Cut away at the tail to release the fillet and then repeat on the other side so you have two fillets that are separated from the bones.

SEAFOOD PREPARATION

Mussels & clams

Preparing mussels and clams is very simple. Ensure that they are alive before you cook them as this means they are fresh and safe for consumption: the shells should be closed, however any shells that are slightly open should shut when tapped or gently pressed. If they remain open, discard them. The same goes for shells which are broken. Only scrub and debeard them just before cooking as mussels don't tend to live for long after this is done.

• Start by rinsing the mussels under cold water and use a gentle scrubbing brush to clean the shells of any seaweed – don't worry if you can't remove tough barnacles.

• Debeard the mussels. This is done by pulling away the small seaweed-like thread that is attached to each mussel – you can use some force and you will feel when it detaches.

• Check again if any of the mussels are open and won't shut when tapped. Discard any of these.

• When the mussels are cooked, discard any that have not opened.

• Clean clams in the same way as mussels, by scrubbing and rinsing the shells. However, clams do not have to be debearded.

Prawns (shrimp)

• Remove the head of the prawn just before it meets the body.

• Carefully remove the shells along the body by peeling them away from the flesh, keeping the prawn intact.

• Along the back of the prawn is where the intestinal tract is – you can usually spot this easily as it is a dark black line. Make a small cut along the back with a knife and carefully pull this away and discard it.

• You can either discard the tails or keep them on for presentation. They can then be discarded when eating the cooked prawns.

• You can also carefully remove the intestinal tract on whole prawns if you wanted to keep them unpeeled for your dish. Simply bend the prawn between the head and the body and use a small knife or cocktail stick to release the tract and remove it.

Scallops

• As with mussels and clams, choose live scallops if you are planning to prepare from the shell. The shells should be shut or, if open, should shut when tapped or pressed. Discard any scallops that remain open or have broken shells. Alternatively you can ask your fishmonger to remove the scallops from the shells for you.

• To deshell, start by holding the scallop by the hinged side and use a table knife to begin to prise it open at the side of the hinge. It will start to open but is held shut by a muscle – scrape under this and around the edge of the shell with the knife to release it.

• One the shell has opened, pull open the two sides fully and discard the empty side.

• Use the same knife to release the scallop from the shell. Then remove the muscle skirting around the edge and the darker membrane. Also ensure you remove and discard the small white ligament attached to the side of the scallop. You should be left with the white scallop meat and the coral attached. Some people choose to remove the coral (it has a stronger flavour, similar to the brown meat in a crab), however it is delicious and completely edible.

COOKING FISH & SEAFOOD

Fish is at its very best when it is just cooked, which rarely takes very long, as it can lose its flavour and become dry when overcooked. It is usually best to use your senses when cooking fish: the fish should flake apart and easily and not be fibrous. When prawns are cooked, they should turn opaque and pink in colour. They will also become firmer in texture.

Deboning cooked whole fish

If you have chosen to cook a whole, round fish, there are simple steps to debone and serve the fish once cooked to ensure you don't waste any of the delicious flesh but that you remove as many bones as possible.

• The whole fish has two fillets with the spine and bone cage in between them, so begin by removing the fillet on the top. Use a table knife to remove the fin bones from the top of the spine.

• Next, make a cut along where the head and fillet meet. Do the same at the end where the fillet meets the tail.

• Cut along the spine, which is in the middle of the fillet and runs down the fish. Pull the top part of the fillet away from the spine, and then do the same with the bottom part. Remove any small bones as you do this. You will then be left with the spine and bone cage on top of the second fillet. Pick this up from the tail end and the whole bone cage can be removed in one (the head usually comes away with this).

• It's worth noting that the flesh in the cheeks of the head is delicious!

BRUNCH & LIGHT BITES

The recipes in this chapter include quicker and lighter meals that would be perfect for a late breakfast or lunch, or as the perfect nibble before a meal. Something simple to whip up for yourself or recipes that will wow your guests.

SPICY SALMON BURGERS WITH SRIRACHA MAYO & PICKLES

These burgers are delicious and make a really fun meal for all ages – substitute beef burgers for these at your next barbecue. The lightly pickled crunchy veg cuts through the spiced sriracha mayo and soft brioche buns.

1 tbsp sriracha
100g (3½oz) mayonnaise
2 tbsp vegetable oil

For the salmon burgers
4 skinless salmon fillets
small handful of coriander (cilantro),
    chopped
2 garlic cloves, crushed
2 spring onions (scallions), chopped
small handful of chives, chopped
1 red chilli, deseeded and finely diced
1 tsp fish sauce

For the pickles
25ml (2 tbsp) rice vinegar
½ tsp caster (superfine) sugar
½ tsp salt
½ cucumber, peeled into ribbons
2 large carrots, peeled into ribbons

To serve
1 baby gem lettuce, leaves separated
    but kept whole
4 brioche burger buns

Place all the ingredients for the burgers into a food processor and pulse the mixture until it resembles a chunky mince. Divide the salmon mixture into four and shape into equal-sized patties. Place them on a tray or plate and transfer to the fridge for 15 minutes to firm up.

While the patties are chilling, make the pickled cucumber and carrot. In a medium bowl mix together the rice vinegar, sugar and salt. Tip the cucumber and carrot ribbons into the bowl and mix well, making sure they are all well coated. Set aside to allow them to lightly pickle.

In a small bowl mix together the mayonnaise and the sriracha.

Now you can fry your salmon burgers. Set a medium non-stick frying pan (skillet) over a medium heat. Drizzle in a little vegetable oil. Fry the salmon patties for 2–3 minutes on each side (you may need to do this in batches). While your burgers are frying, slice the brioche buns in half and lightly toast.

Assemble the burgers: spoon a good dollop of sriracha mayo on the top and bottom of the toasted brioche buns. Place a couple of the lettuce leaves on top, followed by the burger. Top the patty with some of the pickled cucumber and carrots, finishing with the burger bun top.

Serves 4
–
Prep 30 mins
plus chilling
–
Cook 5–6 mins

SALMON & PASTA BROTH WITH WATERCRESS OIL

One-pot cooking at its best! The poaching technique of the salmon ensures super-soft, flaking fish and is a healthy and hearty meal packed full of greens and goodness. Use any small soup pasta you like here.

2 litres (8¾ cups) vegetable stock (bouillon)
125g (4½oz) soup pasta (such as pepe bucato or fregola)
2 skinless salmon fillets
60g (2¼oz) spring greens, shredded
60g (2¼oz) cavolo nero (black kale), shredded
80g (2¾oz) frozen peas
small handful of flat-leaf parsley, roughly chopped
sea salt and freshly ground black pepper
pecorino shavings, to garnish

For the watercress oil
50g (1¾oz) watercress
small handful of basil
50ml (3 tbsp) olive oil

Firstly, make the watercress oil. In a food processor blitz together the watercress, basil and olive oil. Pulse until you have a smooth, green oil. Set to one side while you prepare the broth.

In a large pan add the vegetable stock (bouillon) and bring to the boil. Add the pasta and cook for 3 minutes. After 3 minutes add the salmon fillets, letting them poach in the liquid for approximately 5 minutes. For the final minute or so, add the spring greens, cavolo nero (black kale) and frozen peas and allow them to cook for 1 minute. Once the pasta is tender and the fish is cooked through, stir through the parsley and check the seasoning before removing from the heat.

Spoon into deep bowls, making sure the salmon sits on top (don't worry if it starts to flake apart). Top the bowls with a drizzle of the watercress oil and some pecorino shavings.

Serves 2
–
Prep 10 mins
–
Cook 10 mins

BEETROOT & CARROT FRITTERS WITH FLAKED SALMON

These fritters are beautifully bright in colour and full of the goodness of beetroot (beets) and carrot. The combination of the fritters with the horseradish and salmon makes a lovely brunch or lunch option. It would also work really well with smoked salmon.

2 large carrots, grated
1 beetroot (beet), grated
50g (1¾oz) plain (all-purpose) flour
3 spring onions (scallions), finely
    chopped
½ tsp caraway seeds
small handful of dill, chopped,
    plus extra to garnish
1 egg, beaten
2 skin-on salmon fillets
3 tbsp olive oil, plus extra for drizzling
100g (3½oz) Greek yoghurt
1 tbsp creamed horseradish
1 tsp nigella seeds
sea salt and freshly ground black
    pepper

To serve
½ lemon, cut into wedges

Preheat the oven to 200°C (180°C fan)/400°F/gas 6.

In a large bowl mix together the carrots, beetroot (beet), flour, spring onions (scallions), caraway seeds and dill until evenly incorporated, then season with salt and pepper. Slowly add the beaten egg and mix again (you may not need all the egg). The mixture should be just wet enough that you can shape it into patties in your hands. Shape the mixture into six equal-sized patties.

Line a baking sheet with baking paper, put the salmon fillets onto it, drizzle with olive oil and season with salt and pepper. Bake for 15 minutes until cooked through.

While the fish is cooking, fry your fritters. In a large frying pan (skillet) heat up the olive oil. When the pan is hot, fry your fritters for 2–3 minutes on each side so they are golden brown and crispy (you may need to do this in batches). When cooked, remove from the pan and set onto some paper towels to absorb any excess oil.

In a small bowl mix together the yoghurt with the horseradish and season well.

When the salmon is cooked, discard the skin and gently flake the fish into large pieces.

Serve the fritters with a drizzle of the horseradish yoghurt, some flaked salmon on top and a scattering of extra dill. Sprinkle over the nigella seeds and serve with lemon wedges to squeeze over.

Serves 2
–
Prep 15 mins
–
Cook 20 mins

TUNA POKE BOWLS WITH MISO DRESSING

Poke (which means 'to slice or cut') originates from Hawaii and comprises raw, sushi-grade fish with rice along with a variety of toppings. This poke bowl includes tuna, but you can easily use salmon. Mix and match the toppings if you don't fancy them all, but the umami-packed miso dressing is a must!

200g (7oz) ready-cooked jasmine or
    wholegrain packet rice
2 tsp rice vinegar
200g (7oz) sushi-grade tuna
½ mango, chopped into 1cm (½in)
    cubes
100g (3½oz) fresh (or frozen and
    thawed) edamame beans
½ avocado, thinly sliced
4 radishes, thinly sliced
black and white sesame seeds,
    to garnish

For the pickles
50ml (3 tbsp) rice vinegar
½ tsp salt
½ tsp caster (superfine) sugar
freshly ground black pepper
½ cucumber, peeled into ribbons
1 carrot, cut into matchsticks

For the miso dressing
2 tbsp rice vinegar
1 tbsp white miso paste
1 tsp sesame oil
1 tsp soy sauce
1 tsp runny honey

First, pickle the cucumber and carrot: in a bowl mix together the rice vinegar, salt, sugar and a good grinding of black pepper. Whisk to dissolve the salt and sugar. Add the cucumber and carrots, coating them in the pickling liquid. Place in the fridge for 20–30 minutes while you prepare the rest of the ingredients.

Tip the packet rice into a bowl and break it up, combine it with the rice vinegar and set to one side.

Make the miso dressing: in a small bowl whisk together all the ingredients and set to one side.

Carefully dice the tuna into 1cm (½in) cubes, place them into a bowl and toss with 1 teaspoon of the miso dressing.

Assemble your poke bowls: in two deep, ramen or pasta-style bowls, start by spooning in your rice. Keeping your toppings grouped together in their own little piles, add the seasoned tuna, mango, edamame, avocado and radishes. Spoon into another pile your pickled cucumber and carrot. Finally, drizzle with the remaining miso dressing and sprinkle with the black and white sesame seeds.

Serves 2
–
**Prep 15 mins
plus chilling**

SPEEDY SMOKED MACKEREL PÂTÉ WITH CELERY & APPLE SALAD

This mackerel pâté is so quick to whip up; I often make a big batch at the beginning of the week to dip into for lunches. Simply double the recipe if you want to make more – the pâté will keep for five days in the fridge. Oily fish such as mackerel is high in omega-3, so this is much healthier than meat pâtés.

For the pâté
240g (8½oz) skinless smoked mackerel fillets
zest and juice of 1 lemon
180g (6¼oz) soft cream cheese
small bunch of flat-leaf parsley
½ bunch of dill
1 tsp capers, drained and rinsed
1 tsp wholegrain mustard
sea salt and freshly ground black pepper

For the celery & apple salad
1 tbsp olive oil
1 tbsp lemon juice
3 celery sticks, thinly sliced
2 green apples, cut into matchsticks
½ bunch of dill

To serve
4 slices of bread (sourdough or rye works well)
lemon wedges

To make the pâté: in a food processor, add the smoked mackerel, lemon zest and juice, cream cheese, parsley, dill, capers and wholegrain mustard. Season it well and then pulse together to form a smooth paste. Tip into a bowl and set to one side.

To make the celery and apple salad: in a large bowl whisk together the olive oil and the lemon juice and season well. Add the celery, apple and dill. Toss the salad through the dressing so it is evenly coated.

Use a griddle pan (or a toaster or grill/broiler if you don't have one) to toast the bread.

Serve the warm, griddled toasts with the smoked mackerel pâté, lemon wedges and the crunchy celery and apple salad.

Serves 2
–
Prep 15 mins
–
Cook 2 mins

SMOKED MACKEREL, BEETROOT & RADISH SALAD

This salad is colourful and packed with goodness and flavour. Beetroot (beets) and mackerel work well together, and combined with the bitter chicory (endive), sweet pear and crunchy pine nuts it makes for a delicious lunch or impressive light starter.

2 raw beetroot (beets)
200g (7oz) radishes, halved
drizzle of olive oil
2 chicory (endive), leaves picked and
   shredded
50g (1¾oz) lamb's lettuce or watercress
2 skinless smoked mackerel fillets
   (the peppered fillets work well)
2 firm pears, such as conference,
   sliced lengthways
50g (1¾oz) pine nuts, toasted
sea salt and freshly ground black
   pepper
dill fronds, to garnish

For the vinaigrette dressing
2 tbsp olive oil
1 tbsp lemon juice
1 tsp Dijon mustard
1 tsp runny honey

Preheat the oven to 200°C (180°C fan)/400°F/gas 6.

Start by roasting your beetroot (beets). Wrap them in tin foil, place on a baking tin and bake for 30 minutes. After 15 minutes add the radishes to the tin around the foiled beetroot and drizzle them with some oil and seasoning. Return to the oven and roast for a further 15 minutes. The beetroot should be tender when inserted with a knife. Open the foil and allow them to cool slightly.

While the beetroot and radishes are cooking, prepare the dressing. In a small bowl, whisk together the olive oil, lemon juice, Dijon mustard and honey. In a large bowl add the shredded chicory (endive) and lamb's lettuce or watercress and toss them in some of the dressing, reserving some to drizzle at the end.

Flake the mackerel fillets. Remove the skin from the beetroot – it should peel away easily, but you might want to wear gloves as they can stain your hands. Cut the beetroot into neat wedges.

Assemble the salad: pile the dressed salad leaves onto the plates. Scatter over the beetroot wedges, pear slices, roasted radishes and flaked mackerel. Top with the toasted pine nuts, an extra drizzle of the dressing and some dill.

Serves 2
–
Prep 10 mins
–
Cook 30 mins

SMOKED HADDOCK FISHCAKES, SPINACH & EGGS

These smoked haddock fishcakes, served with a runny poached egg, are perfect for a special brunch. You can make the fishcakes in advance and have them chilling in the fridge until you're ready to fry them. Alternatively, you could serve these for dinner alongside some greens of your choice.

350g (12oz) floury potatoes (such as Maris Pipers), peeled and roughly chopped
knob of butter
1 white onion, finely chopped
300g (10½oz) skin-on smoked haddock fillets
zest of 1 lemon
1 tsp wholegrain mustard
10g (¼oz) chives, finely chopped
50g (1¾oz) plain (all-purpose) flour
1 large egg, beaten
70g (2½oz) stale white breadcrumbs
2 tbsp vegetable oil
sea salt and freshly ground black pepper

To serve
100g (3½oz) spinach
knob of butter
2 eggs
cracked black pepper
chives, very finely chopped

Place the potatoes in a large pan of cold, salted water. Bring to a boil then reduce to a simmer and allow the potatoes to cook for 15–20 minutes until tender. Drain and mash or put through a ricer to get a smoother mash. Set aside.

Add a knob of butter to a frying pan (skillet) set over a medium–low heat and allow it to melt. Once the butter is foaming, add the onion and fry until soft, translucent and beginning to turn golden. Take off the heat and set aside.

Place the smoked haddock in a shallow pan and fill with water until the fillets are just covered. Simmer on a gentle heat for 4 minutes until the fish is just cooked through. Remove from the heat and drain off the water. Allow the fish to cool slightly so it's easier to handle, and then remove the skin and any small bones. Flake the fish into chunks.

In a large bowl, mix the fried onion with the mashed potato. Stir through the lemon zest, mustard, chives and plenty of seasoning. Fold through the flaked fish and shape the mixture into four fishcakes. Place them on a lined baking sheet or plate and refrigerate for 20 minutes to firm up.

After 20 minutes, remove the fishcakes from the fridge. Place the flour in a small bowl, the beaten egg in another and the breadcrumbs in a third bowl. Coat the fishcakes one at a time: dust in flour, then beaten egg, followed by breadcrumbs, ensuring that the crumbs are pressed on really well so they stick. Repeat until all the fishcakes are coated.

Place a large, non-stick frying pan over a medium heat and drizzle in some oil. Fry the fishcakes for 4–5 minutes on each side until they are golden brown and cooked through.

While the fishcakes are frying, cook some spinach in a pan with a splash of water, a knob of butter and plenty of seasoning until just wilted. Cook two poached eggs until perfectly runny in the middle.

When all the elements are ready, serve up: top a golden, crispy fishcake (or two, depending on how hungry you are) with some wilted spinach, followed by a poached egg. Garnish with cracked black pepper and chopped chives.

Serves 2
–
Prep 45 mins plus chilling
–
Cook 30 mins

SMOKED HADDOCK SCOTCH EGGS WITH MAYO

A step up from the pub scotch egg! If you do your timings correctly with this you will achieve perfectly runny yolks in the eggs, encased in crispy, golden breadcrumbs. Served alongside the homemade tarragon mayonnaise, this is an impressive dinner-party starter.

300g (10½oz) floury potatoes (such as Maris Pipers), peeled and chopped
knob of butter
240g (8½oz) skinless smoked haddock
15g (½oz) flat-leaf parsley, finely chopped
10g (¼oz) dill, finely chopped
1 tsp wholegrain mustard
6 eggs
100g (3½oz) plain (all-purpose) flour
150g (5½oz) panko breadcrumbs
vegetable oil, for frying
sea salt and freshly ground black pepper

For the mayo
1 egg yolk
1 tsp Dijon mustard
500ml (2 cups) rapeseed oil
juice of ½ lemon
1 tsp sherry vinegar
small bunch of tarragon, leaves chopped

To serve
watercress leaves

Serves 4
–
Prep 30 mins
plus chilling
–
Cook 30 mins

You need the mashed potato to be cold, so it's often easier to make this ahead of time. Put the potatoes in a large pan and cover with cold, salted water. Bring to the boil, then simmer for 15–20 minutes until tender. Drain and mash. Stir through the butter and season. Set aside to cool, then refrigerate.

Make the mayo: in a large bowl, whisk together the egg yolk with the mustard. Slowly drizzle in the oil in a steady stream, whisking continuously. The mixture will thicken and turn glossy. Add the lemon juice and vinegar and mix again. Stir through the tarragon, add some seasoning and set aside.

In a food processor, add the smoked haddock and 300g (10½oz) of mashed potato. Pulse until fairly smooth. Tip into a large bowl and mix through the herbs, mustard and plenty of seasoning. Place in the fridge.

In a large pan of gently simmering water, boil four of your eggs for precisely 6 minutes before removing with a slotted spoon and plunging immediately into a bowl of iced water – this ensures you will have runny yolks! Allow to cool completely before carefully peeling (do this gently to avoid breaking them). Take a spoonful of the haddock mash and spread it across the palm of your hand. Place one of the peeled eggs in the middle and carefully enclose the egg by closing your palm and covering with the mash. Press the mixture around the egg so it is completely coated and there are no air pockets. Repeat with the other three eggs.

Get three small bowls ready: one with the flour, one with the two remaining eggs (beaten) and one with the breadcrumbs. Coat each scotch egg in the flour first, dusting off any excess, then in the beaten egg, then in the breadcrumbs (making sure they are well coated). Repeat with all the eggs.

Pour vegetable oil into a large, high-sided pan to come halfway up. Heat the oil until it reaches 180°C (355°F). If you don't have a thermometer, drop in a small piece of bread – it should sizzle and turn golden if the oil is hot enough. Use a slotted spoon to lower in the scotch eggs in batches and fry for 6 minutes until golden brown on all sides. Remove with the slotted spoon and place on paper towels to drain. Serve alongside the mayo and some peppery watercress.

GOAN MASALA MACKEREL & KACHUMBER SALAD

The blended spice paste stuffed inside the mackerel fillets really packs a punch and marries perfectly with the oily fish. Kachumber, or cachumber, is an Indian salad that consists of tomato, red onion and spices and is perfect alongside the fish.

2 small skin-on mackerel, cut into
    4 fillets
100g (3½oz) plain (all-purpose) flour
3 tbsp vegetable oil
sea salt and freshly ground black
    pepper

For the masala paste
1 tsp cumin seeds
3 tsp coriander seeds
1 tsp black peppercorns
½ tsp cloves
1 tsp ground turmeric
1 tsp garam masala
2 tsp chilli (red pepper) flakes
1 tsp flaky salt
4 garlic cloves, chopped
40g (1½oz) ginger, peeled and chopped
1 tsp tamarind paste
3 tbsp red wine vinegar

For the kachumber salad
2 tsp white wine vinegar
¼ tsp ground cumin
pinch of salt
pinch of smoked paprika
200g tomatoes (green, yellow or red),
    sliced
½ red onion, thinly sliced
small handful of coriander (cilantro),
    leaves picked and finely chopped

To serve
flatbreads
natural (plain) yoghurt

Firstly, make the masala paste: grind the cumin, coriander, peppercorns and cloves in a pestle and mortar until you have a powder. Tip this into a food processor and blitz along with the turmeric, garam masala, chilli (red pepper) flakes, salt, garlic, ginger, tamarind paste and red wine vinegar to form a smooth paste.

Spread 1 heaped teaspoon of the masala paste on the flesh side of one of the fillets and then sandwich the other fillet on top (flesh-side down). Use some kitchen string to bind the halves together. Repeat with the other two fillets.

Prepare the kachumber salad by whisking together the vinegar, cumin, salt and paprika. Add the tomatoes, red onion and coriander (cilantro) and toss together.

In a shallow bowl, add the plain (all-purpose) flour and season it well with salt and pepper. Heat the vegetable oil in a large, wide pan set over a medium heat. Carefully coat both stuffed mackerel in the flour and tap off any excess. Fry them in the hot oil for 3 minutes on each side until they are golden and crispy.

Serve the stuffed mackerel alongside the tomato kachumber salad, some warmed flatbreads and a dollop of yoghurt.

Serves 4–6
—
Prep 30 mins
—
Cook 10 mins

MISO & TAHINI-BAKED COD WITH NOODLES & GINGER VEG

Miso and tahini marry to create the most delicious, umami-packed crust for the delicate cod. Served with soba noodles and Asian fried greens and mushrooms, it makes a delicious and healthy dinner.

2 skinless cod fillets
120g (4¼oz) soba noodles
1 tbsp sesame oil, plus a drizzle
thumb-sized piece of ginger, peeled and finely chopped
80g (2¾oz) tenderstem broccoli
2 pak choi (bok choy), halved lengthways
80g (2¾oz) shiitake mushrooms
1 tbsp soy sauce
1 tbsp toasted sesame seeds
small handful of coriander (cilantro) leaves

For the marinade
2 tbsp white miso paste
1 tbsp tahini
1 tbsp soy sauce
1 tbsp mirin
1 tsp runny honey
1 tsp toasted sesame oil

Preheat the oven to 200°C (180°C fan)/400°F/gas 6.

In a small bowl, mix together the marinade ingredients. Coat the cod fillets in the marinade and then place into a baking tin. Drizzle over any remaining marinade and then place into the middle of the oven to bake for 20 minutes.

While the fish is baking, cook the soba noodles according to the packet instructions. Toss them in a little sesame oil after cooking to avoid them sticking together.

In a large frying pan (skillet) set over a medium–high heat, heat up some sesame oil and add the ginger and broccoli. Fry for a minute before adding the shiitake and pak choi (bok choy). Continue to fry until the vegetables begin to soften. Add the soy sauce and allow it to cook and sizzle for a further minute. Remove from the heat.

To serve, pile the noodles into a bowl, top with some of the ginger-fried vegetables and add the miso-tahini cod on top. Drizzle over any remaining juices from the baking tin. Garnish with the toasted sesame seeds and some coriander (cilantro) leaves.

Serves 2
–
Prep 10 mins
–
Cook 25 mins

CRAB SALAD WITH FENNEL, ASPARAGUS & COURGETTE

This raw, shaved salad is wonderfully fresh and perfect on a summer's day. The crispy, crunchy vegetables marry with the crab and punchy ponzu dressing (but don't worry if you can't find ponzu, you can use lime juice instead).

1 fennel bulb
100g (3½oz) asparagus, woody stalks discarded
1 courgette (zucchini)
80g (2¾oz) sugar snap peas, thinly sliced
100g (3½oz) white crabmeat
1 tsp black sesame seeds
small handful of dill, to garnish

For the dressing
2 tbsp ponzu or lime juice
1 tsp Dijon mustard
1 tsp sesame oil
4 tbsp rapeseed oil
pinch of caster (superfine) sugar

Begin by thinly slicing the fennel and courgette (zucchini) for the salad – if you have a mandoline then this works best, but alternatively you can thinly slice with a knife. To slice the asparagus, use a peeler to create ribbons.

Prepare the salad dressing by whisking together the ponzu or lime juice, mustard, sesame oil, rapeseed oil and sugar in a small bowl until smooth.

Scatter the sliced vegetables onto a serving platter and distribute the crabmeat around the salad. Drizzle over the dressing and then top with a sprinkling of black sesame seeds and dill.

Serves 2
–
Prep 15 mins

WARM SCALLOP SALAD WITH GREENS & CRISPY PROSCIUTTO

This salad is a classic combination of flavours and the minted peas work brilliantly with the scallops. Cooking prosciutto in the oven results in crispy, salty and deliciously moreish pieces to top salads with. This dish is great when hosting, as it requires minimal effort but looks and tastes impressive.

4 slices of prosciutto
150g (5½oz) green beans
100g (3½oz) mangetout (snow peas)
250g (9oz) frozen peas
1 tbsp olive oil
6 scallops
25g (1oz) butter
handful of mint, leaves picked and roughly chopped
sea salt and freshly ground black pepper
pea shoots, to garnish
extra virgin olive oil, to garnish

Preheat the oven to 200°C (180°C fan)/400°F/gas 6.

Place the prosciutto slices onto a baking sheet lined with baking paper and bake in the middle of the oven for about 10 minutes until they are crispy.

While the prosciutto is cooking, put a pan of water on to boil. Once boiling add the green beans and mangetout (snow peas) for 1 minute, then pour in the frozen peas and continue to blanch for a further minute before draining both.

Heat up a griddle pan. Rub olive oil and seasoning all over the scallops. When the griddle pan is nice and hot, cook the scallops for 1–2 minutes on each side – you want to achieve char lines but not overcook the scallops. Once cooked, remove from the pan.

In a small pan, melt the butter and once foamy add the green beans and peas and season well. Add the chopped mint, tossing with the greens in the butter for 2 minutes.

Spoon the minted greens onto the plates, top with the seared scallops and then break up the crispy prosciutto into pieces over the top. Garnish with some pea shoots and a drizzle of extra virgin olive oil.

Serves 2
–
Prep 10 mins
–
Cook 15 mins

PRAWN TOAST

Prawn (shrimp) toast is a firm favourite for many when ordering a takeaway. This version is packed full of fresh prawns and despite being fried, is surprisingly light. You will never want to go back to the takeaway version again!

400g (14oz) raw, peeled prawns (shrimp)
1 garlic clove, roughly chopped
5cm (2in) piece of ginger, peeled and grated
2 spring onions (scallions), chopped
1 tsp soy sauce
1 tsp cornflour (cornstarch)
4 slices of white bread, crusts removed
2 tbsp white sesame seeds
2 tbsp black sesame seeds
vegetable oil, for frying

To serve
sweet chilli or soy sauce

In a food processor, blitz together the prawns (shrimp), garlic, ginger, spring onions (scallions), soy sauce and cornflour (cornstarch) – the mixture should be fairly smooth but still have a little texture.

Take a slice of the white bread and press on a quarter of the prawn mixture, pressing it down firmly so it sticks on, and making sure it is spread all the way to the edges. In a shallow bowl, mix together the white and black sesame seeds. Press the bread prawn-side down into the sesame seeds so it coats it. Repeat with the other slices.

In a high-sided pan, add the vegetable oil so it comes 3cm (1¼in) up the sides. Heat the oil until it reaches 180°C (355°F. If you don't have a thermometer, test the temperature with a small piece of bread – when it sizzles and turns golden brown then it is ready. Cooking in batches, start with the prawn side of the bread and fry for 2–3 minutes and then turn in the oil and fry the other side. They should be golden brown, crispy and with the prawn cooked through.

Remove the toasts from the oil and set onto paper towels to absorb any excess oil.

To serve, cut the toasts in half diagonally and dip into sweet chilli sauce or soy sauce.

Serves 4
–
Prep 15 mins
–
Cook 5 mins

PRAWN NOODLE LETTUCE CUPS WITH SATAY SAUCE

These tasty little lettuce cups make a lovely and exciting canapé or nibble. Inspired by Vietnamese summer rolls, these are much easier to prepare but provide the same delicious flavours. Serve on a warm day with cold drinks on hand.

100g (3½oz) vermicelli noodles
2 tbsp sesame oil
1 tbsp honey
thumb-sized piece of ginger, peeled and grated
1 tbsp sesame seeds
zest of 1 lime
150g (5½oz) raw, peeled king prawns (jumbo shrimp)
2 baby gem lettuces
½ cucumber, cut into thin matchsticks
handful of Thai basil, leaves picked
small handful of mint, leaves picked
40g (1½oz) crispy onions
1 chilli, finely diced

For the satay sauce
3 tbsp smooth peanut butter
1 tbsp soy sauce
1 tsp runny honey
juice of ½ lime
1 tsp sriracha
1 tsp curry powder
170ml (scant ¾ cup) coconut milk

Start by cooking the vermicelli noodles according to the packet instructions. Once cooked, drain and run them under cold water until they are cool. Put them into a bowl and toss with 1 tablespoon of sesame oil (this will help to stop them from sticking together).

In a small bowl, whisk together the ingredients for the satay sauce and set aside. Pull apart the leaves of the gem lettuce so you have little 'cups' that you can fill.

In another small bowl, mix together the honey, ginger, sesame seeds, lime zest and the remaining 1 tablespoon of sesame oil. Add the prawns (shrimp) to the bowl and toss them so they are evenly coated. Heat a frying pan (skillet) over a medium heat and then add the prawns, turning and cooking them evenly for about 2 minutes on each side. They will turn pink when cooked and get a golden glaze from the honey. Remove the prawns from the pan.

Bring a big serving platter to the table with the lettuce cups, noodles, sesame-coated prawns, cucumber, fresh herbs and crispy onions. Pile these into the lettuce cups, then drizzle over the satay sauce and top with the red chilli.

Serves 4
–
Prep 20 mins
–
Cook 10 mins

PRAWN & KIMCHI FRIED RICE WITH CRISPY EGGS

The combination of the fermented kimchi, sweet and spicy prawns (shrimp), fried rice and crispy egg work perfectly here. This is a great quick lunch option and is also the perfect cure for a hangover!

1 tbsp sesame oil
100g (3½oz) kimchi, roughly chopped
1 tsp gochujang paste
200g (7oz) raw, peeled prawns (shrimp)
150g (5½oz) cooked jasmine rice
2 tbsp groundnut oil
2 eggs
2 spring onions (scallions), finely sliced
1 sheet of nori seaweed, cut into thin strips
1 tsp black sesame seeds
coriander (cilantro) leaves, to garnish
chilli oil – I use Lee Kum Kee Chiu Chow Chilli Oil (optional)

Pour the sesame oil into a medium frying pan (skillet) set over a medium heat. Once hot, add the kimchi and gochujang paste and fry for 2 minutes. Next add the prawns (shrimp) and cooked rice and stir-fry together for 3 minutes.

While the prawns and rice are frying, put a separate small, non-stick frying pan over a high heat. Add 1 tablespoon of groundnut oil and, when hot, crack in your eggs. Keep frying and add an additional 1 tablespoon of oil around the edges to achieve a crispy 'skirt' of egg whites, but still with a runny yolk. Once cooked, remove from the heat.

Stir the spring onions (scallions) through the kimchi prawn rice and then tip into bowls. Top each with a crispy fried egg, nori strips, sesame seeds and some coriander (cilantro) leaves. Finish with a drizzle of chilli oil, if desired.

Serves 2
–
Prep 5 mins
–
Cook 10 mins

PRAWNS WITH WATERMELON, AVOCADO & HALLOUMI

This salad is refreshing, light and full of zesty flavours. The watermelon, prawns (shrimp) and halloumi work really well together, and this would make an ideal salad to serve on a warm summer's day in the garden.

4 spring onions (scallions)
250g (9oz) halloumi, cut into slices
1 tbsp sesame oil, plus extra for
   brushing
200g (7oz) raw, tail-on tiger prawns
   (shrimp), shells removed
1 watermelon (approximately 700g/1lb
   9oz), cut into small wedges
1 red chilli, deseeded and finely
   chopped
handful of mint, leaves picked
100g (3½oz) toasted cashews, chopped
1 tbsp toasted sesame seeds
2 avocados, thinly sliced

For the lime dressing
zest and juice of 1 lime
2 tbsp sesame oil
1 tbsp soy sauce
½ tsp fish sauce
1 tsp runny honey
1 tbsp coriander (cilantro), finely
   chopped

In a small bowl, whisk together all the ingredients for the lime dressing.

Cut the spring onions (scallions) into thin strips lengthways and put them into a small bowl or glass of iced water – this will make them curl, creating lovely decorative coils.

Heat up a griddle pan and brush both sides of the halloumi slices with some sesame oil. Once the pan is hot, griddle the halloumi for 3 minutes on each side, creating char lines.

In a frying pan (skillet) heat up 1 tablespoon of sesame oil. Add the prawns (shrimp) and stir-fry for 2–3 minutes until the prawns are cooked through. Remove them from the pan and set aside.

Get a large salad bowl and add the watermelon wedges, red chilli, mint leaves, cashews, sesame seeds and spring onion curls. Pour over half the dressing and toss so everything is well coated. Top with the sliced avocado, prawns and halloumi. Drizzle over the remaining dressing and serve.

Serves 4
–
Prep 15 mins
–
Cook 10 mins

CORONATION PRAWN BUNS

This super-quick and easy take on coronation chicken uses prawns instead, and requires very little prep. Make up the mixture and pop it in an airtight container for a perfect picnic sandwich-filler.

250g (9oz) cooked, peeled prawns
   (shrimp)
4 brioche finger buns or hot dog buns
50g (1¾oz) rocket (arugula)
1 baby cucumber, thinly sliced
1 tsp nigella seeds
sea salt and freshly ground black
   pepper

For the coronation dressing
3 tbsp mayonnaise
3 tbsp natural (plain) yoghurt
2 tbsp mango chutney, plus extra
   to serve
2 tsp curry powder
small handful of chives, chopped

In a bowl, mix together all the ingredients for the coronation dressing. Season well and stir through the cooked, peeled prawns (shrimp).

Cut the buns lengthways but not the whole way through. Spoon in the prawn filling, along with some rocket (arugula) and cucumber slices. Sprinkle over some nigella seeds and serve immediately.

Serves 4
—
Prep 15 mins

PEA & AVOCADO SMASH WITH POLENTA PRAWNS

Smashed avocado on toast is an established favourite for brunches and lunches. This recipe elevates the classic with crunchy crusted prawns (shrimp), feta and chilli, which is a great combination and incredibly easy to throw together.

1 large ripe avocado
50g (1¾oz) frozen peas, thawed in boiling water then drained
juice of 1 lime
small handful of coriander (cilantro), chopped
100g (3½oz) fine polenta
pinch of chilli (red pepper) flakes
100g (3½oz) raw, peeled king prawns (jumbo shrimp)
1 tbsp olive oil, plus extra to drizzle
2 slices of sourdough bread, toasted
50g (1¾oz) feta cheese, crumbled
1 spring onion (scallion), finely sliced
½ red chilli, deseeded and finely diced
small handful of pea shoots (optional)
sea salt and freshly ground black pepper

To serve
1 lime, cut into wedges

Mash the avocado flesh with the back of a fork, leaving it slightly chunky. Keep some of the peas whole but mash the rest in the same way as the avocado and then stir them together. Add the lime juice, coriander (cilantro) and some seasoning.

In a shallow bowl, mix together the polenta with the chilli (red pepper) flakes and some seasoning. Toss and coat the prawns (shrimp) in the polenta mix. Pour 1 tablespoon of olive oil into a large frying pan (skillet) over a medium heat. When hot, fry the coated prawns for 1–2 minutes on each side until they are just cooked through and turning golden. Remove from the heat.

Top the toasted sourdough slices with the avocado and pea smash, then add some of the polenta-crusted prawns. Crumble over some feta, spring onion (scallion) and diced chilli. Finish with a drizzle of olive oil, some pea shoots, if using, and lime wedges for squeezing over.

Serves 2
–
Prep 15 mins
–
Cook 5 mins

PORK & PRAWN CRISPY GYOZA WITH DIPPING SAUCE

Pork and prawns (shrimp) are a classic combination for a gyoza filling – the fat content from the pork results in a juicy and tender middle. If you don't eat meat, you can easily make these with just prawns and double the amount. These are so moreish you won't be able to stop eating them!

200g (7oz) raw, peeled prawns (shrimp), finely chopped
180g (6¼oz) pork mince (ground pork)
1 red chilli, deseeded and finely diced
5cm (2in) piece of ginger, peeled and grated
3 garlic cloves, grated
3 spring onions (scallions), finely chopped
70g (2½oz) water chestnuts, finely chopped
10g (¼oz) coriander (cilantro), finely chopped
10g (¼oz) chives, finely chopped
1 tbsp oyster sauce
1 tsp soy sauce
20 (or thereabouts) gyoza wrappers (these can be found at most Asian supermarkets)
2 tbsp vegetable oil

For the dipping sauce
2 tsp rice vinegar
1 tsp mirin
1 tbsp soy sauce
1 tsp crispy chilli oil
1 tsp caster (superfine) sugar

In a large bowl, combine the prawns (shrimp), pork, chilli, ginger, garlic, spring onions (scallions), water chestnuts, coriander (cilantro), chives, oyster sauce and soy sauce. Mix thoroughly to combine.

Place a small bowl of cold water next to you and take a gyoza wrapper in the palm of your hand. Spoon 1 heaped teaspoon of the dumpling mixture into the middle of the wrapper and then dip your finger in the water and run it around half of the edge of the wrapper. Fold the wrapper to encase the dumpling filling, and then use your fingers to crimp the edges around the seam. Make sure to really press well to seal it so that the filling doesn't fall out when cooking. Repeat until you have used up all your filling.

Set a large pan with a tight-fitting lid over a medium heat and add the vegetable oil. Once the oil is hot, add the dumplings on the non-crimped side and fry the bottoms for 2–3 minutes until golden brown and crispy. Then add a splash of water to the pan and place the lid on quickly (it will spit and splutter). Allow the dumplings to steam with the lid on for 3 minutes.

Mix the ingredients for the dipping sauce together in a small bowl and serve with dumplings.

Serves 4–6
–
Prep 30 mins
–
Cook 10 mins

CRISPY SALT & PEPPER SQUID WITH HARISSA MAYO

Calamari is loved by so many and instantly transports you to holidays by the sea. This salt and pepper version has Asian flavours and makes a brilliant nibble to serve with drinks.

600g baby squid
50g (1¾oz) plain (all-purpose) flour
50g (1¾oz) cornflour (cornstarch)
½ tsp salt
1 tsp black pepper
vegetable oil, for frying
100g (3½oz) mayonnaise
1 tsp harissa
2 lemons, cut into wedges

For the marinade
2 tbsp Shaoxing wine
1 tsp soy sauce
5cm (2in) piece of ginger, peeled and grated
2 garlic cloves, grated

Prepare the squid: make sure the wings are removed and discarded, then cut off the tentacles, leaving them whole. Rinse under water. Cut the body into rings or thick slices and score carefully with a knife to create a crisscross pattern. In a large bowl, mix together the marinade ingredients, toss in the squid and place in the fridge for 15 minutes.

In another large bowl, mix together both flours with the salt and pepper. Pour the vegetable oil in a large, high-sided pan to come 8cm (3in) up the sides. Start heating the oil.

Remove the squid from its marinade and toss into the seasoned flour, ensuring that all the pieces are well coated.

When the oil has reached 180°C (355°F), you are ready to fry (if you don't have a thermometer, you can test the temperature by dropping in a small piece of bread – if it sizzles and turns golden then it is ready). Use a spider or slotted spoon to lower the coated squid into the oil. Let them fry for 2–3 minutes until golden brown and crispy. Remove from the oil and drain on some paper towels.

Mix together the mayonnaise and harissa and serve with the crispy squid and some lemon wedges to squeeze over.

Serves 4
–
Prep 15 mins
plus marinating
–
Cook 5 mins

QUICK
& EASY

Seafood often tastes its very best when cooked quickly and these simple, speedy recipes won't disappoint in flavour and variety.

COD GOUJONS, SWEET POTATO WEDGES & HERBY YOGHURT

These goujons are just like a fancy fish finger. The crunchy golden breadcrumbs keep the fish inside incredibly moist, and they are a great way to introduce fish to fussy eaters. Omit the sweet potato wedges and sandwich these between two slices of white bread for the ultimate fish-finger butty!

100g (3½oz) plain (all-purpose) flour
200g (7oz) panko breadcrumbs
zest of 1 lemon
15g (½oz) flat-leaf parsley, finely
    chopped
1 egg, beaten
4 skinless cod fillets, sliced into
    2½cm (1in) pieces
vegetable oil, for frying
sea salt and freshly ground black
    pepper

For the herby yoghurt
200g (7oz) Greek yoghurt
1 tbsp capers, drained and rinsed
4 cornichons, finely chopped
10g (¼oz) dill, chopped
zest and juice of ½ lemon

For the sweet potato wedges
3 large sweet potatoes
1 tbsp olive oil
½ tsp smoked paprika

To serve
watercress or rocket (arugula) salad
½ lemon, cut into wedges

Preheat the oven to 200°C (180°C fan)/400°F/gas 6.

Add all the ingredients for the herby yoghurt to a bowl, along with plenty of seasoning. Mix together and set aside.

Slice the sweet potatoes into long wedges, keeping the skin on. In a large bowl, mix together the olive oil and smoked paprika and season with salt and pepper. Add the sweet potatoes to the bowl and toss them so all the wedges are evenly coated. Tip them onto a large baking sheet, spreading them out evenly, then place into the middle of the oven to cook for 20 minutes, turning them halfway through.

Meanwhile, prepare the goujons. Gather three separate bowls: in the first add the flour, seasoning it really well with salt and pepper. In the second, mix the panko breadcrumbs, lemon zest and parsley. To the final bowl, add the beaten egg. Have a plate or tray ready to put your coated fish goujons on. Take a piece of fish and firstly toss in the flour, shaking off any excess so it's evenly coated. Next place it in the egg bowl, again coating evenly but allowing the excess to drip off. Finally toss in the breadcrumbs, making sure it is well crusted by pressing the crumbs into the fish. Place each piece onto the plate or tray as you continue to coat the rest.

In a large, high-sided pan, heat up 10cm (4in) of vegetable oil. If you have a thermometer, heat the oil to 180°C (355°F). If you don't, test if the oil is hot enough by dropping in a small piece of bread or some breadcrumbs – you want it to sizzle and turn golden brown. Once the oil is hot enough, fry the goujons in batches, for approximately 4 minutes each until they are crispy and golden brown. Remove them from the hot oil using a slotted spoon and place them onto some paper towels to absorb any excess oil.

Serve the crispy, crunchy goujons alongside the sweet potato wedges, herby yoghurt, peppery green salad and some lemon wedges for squeezing.

Serves 4
–
Prep 25 mins
–
Cook 25 mins

BAKED, HERB-CRUSTED COD WITH TOMATO & CHICKPEAS

This is a simple, one-pot meal which is quick and easy to throw together. The sweet, roasted tomatoes create a thick sauce that marries beautifully with the herb-crusted cod.

3 tbsp olive oil
2 garlic cloves, crushed
25g (1oz) Parmesan, grated
small handful of flat-leaf parsley, roughly chopped
small of handful chives, roughly chopped
25g (1oz) fresh breadcrumbs
2 skinless cod fillets
sea salt and freshly ground black pepper

For the tomato & chickpeas
glug of olive oil
1 onion, chopped
2 garlic cloves, sliced
½ tsp fennel seeds
½ tsp chilli (red pepper) flakes
400g (14oz) tin chopped tomatoes
150g (5½oz) cherry tomatoes, halved
1 tsp sherry vinegar
few sprigs of thyme, leaves picked, plus extra to garnish
400g (14oz) tin chickpeas (garbanzo beans), drained and rinsed

To serve
greens or crusty bread

Preheat the oven to 200°C (180°C fan)/400°F/gas 6.

For the tomato and chickpeas, place a large, shallow casserole dish or large, oven-safe frying pan (skillet) over a medium heat and add a glug of olive oil. Once the oil has heated up, add the onion and a pinch of salt, and fry for a few minutes until softened and beginning to turn translucent. Add the garlic and allow to fry for another 2 minutes. Next add the fennel seeds and chilli (red pepper) flakes and fry with the onion and garlic for a minute or so until fragrant. Pour in the tinned tomatoes, cherry tomatoes, sherry vinegar and thyme leaves. Bring to a boil and then reduce the heat and allow to simmer for 10 minutes while you prepare the fish.

In a food processor, add the olive oil, garlic cloves, Parmesan, parsley and chives along with some seasoning. Pulse until you have a vibrant green, chunky paste. Stir through the breadcrumbs.

After the tomatoes have bubbled away and reduced for 10 minutes, add the chickpeas (garbanzo beans) and stir through. Spread both cod fillets with a generous topping of the herb crust, pressing it into the fish, and then sit them on top of the tomato and chickpea sauce. Place the pan on the middle shelf of the oven and cook for 10 minutes.

Once cooked, garnish with some thyme sprigs. Serve alongside some greens or crusty bread to mop up all the sauce and juices.

Serves 2
—
Prep 15 mins
—
Cook 25 mins

Quick & Easy

GRIDDLED SUMAC TUNA WITH WILD RICE & SALSA

This recipe is a great way to mix up any midweek cooking rut you might be in. Using tinned pineapple instead of fresh means the ingredient list is accessible and quicker to assemble. You could also substitute the tuna for a white fish fillet, but pineapple pairs particularly well with meaty tuna.

120g (4¼oz) mixed wholegrain and wild rice
2 tuna steaks
2 tbsp olive oil
1 tsp sumac
sea salt and freshly ground black pepper
lime wedges, to serve

For the salsa
200g (7oz) tin pineapple, diced
1 red chilli, finely chopped
1 small avocado, diced
1 small tomato, diced
40g (1½oz) black beans, drained and rinsed
juice of 1 lime
25g (1oz) coriander (cilantro), chopped

Cook the wild rice according to its packet instructions.

While the rice is cooking, prepare the salsa. Combine the diced pineapple, red chilli, avocado, tomato and black beans in a large bowl. Stir through the pineapple juice, lime juice and half the chopped coriander (cilantro). Check the seasoning and set to one side.

Put a griddle pan over a medium–high heat. Rub the tuna steaks on both sides with olive oil and coat with the sumac and some seasoning. When you have drained and fluffed up the cooked rice with a fork, stir through the remaining chopped coriander and set to one side with the lid on to keep warm.

Once the griddle pan is hot, add the tuna steaks. Allow them to cook for 2 minutes before turning and cooking for 2 minutes on the other side. Once cooked, remove from the pan.

To serve, start with a bed of the coriander rice, place a griddled tuna steak on top and then spoon over some of the salsa. Top with some coriander leaves and lime wedges on the side.

Serves 2
–
Prep 10 mins
–
Cook 10 mins

Quick & Easy

SEA BASS CEVICHE WITH CORN TORTILLA CHIPS

Ceviche originates from Peru, where fresh, raw fish is cured in citrus juices. It is simple to prepare, elegant and refreshing. This recipe uses orange, chilli, lime and yuzu (optional) to give a vibrant flavour to the sea bass. Take time to carefully slice the ingredients as this adds to the refinement.

4 very fresh, skinless sea bass fillets
1 small red onion, finely sliced
3 or 4 radishes, finely sliced
¼ cucumber, finely diced
1 red chilli, finely diced
small handful of coriander (cilantro), leaves picked
sea salt

For the marinade
3 limes, zest of 1 and juice of 3
thumb-sized piece of ginger, peeled and grated
2 garlic cloves, grated
1 tsp yuzu juice (optional)
1 large orange or 2 blood oranges

For the tortilla chips
6 corn tortillas
2 tbsp vegetable oil
1 tsp flaky sea salt
1 tsp Aleppo pepper (optional)

Preheat the oven to 200°C (180°C fan)/400°F/gas 6.

Make the tortilla chips: brush each side of the tortillas with the vegetable oil and cut them into six or eight triangles, depending on their size. Spread these out in an even layer on a large baking sheet lined with baking paper and sprinkle with sea salt and Aleppo pepper. Bake in the oven for about 5 minutes or until lightly golden brown and crisp, then set to one side.

Finely slice the sea bass fillets across the grain and season well with salt. In a large bowl, mix together the lime zest and juice, ginger, garlic and yuzu. Peel the orange (or oranges) and cut into segments over the bowl so the juices drain into the marinade. Squeeze out any remaining juice into the bowl and set the orange segments to one side. Mix the marinade together well and then add the fish slices to it. Leave this to cure for 10–15 minutes, until the fish turns opaque.

Place the red onion slices in a bowl and pour over some boiling water to soften them and make them less raw. Leave them for 3–5 minutes before draining.

Now you can assemble the ceviche. Arrange the fish slices on a serving platter. Top with the orange segments and softened onion slices. Scatter over the radishes, cucumber and chilli. Garnish with the coriander (cilantro) leaves and serve alongside the tortilla chips.

> Serves 4
> –
> Prep 20 mins
> –
> Cook 10 mins

STEAMED HALIBUT WITH HERBY SPELT SALAD

Steaming fish is one of the healthiest ways of cooking it, and using a parcel technique like this means the fish cooks with all the juices and flavours of the other ingredients. Spelt is an ancient grain and contains wholegrain benefits – it is packed full of protein and also has a wonderfully nutty flavour.

½ fennel bulb, thinly sliced
2 skin-on halibut fillets
1 orange, peeled and sliced in rounds
25g (1oz) pitted black olives, halved
small handful of flat-leaf parsley,
    roughly chopped
2 tbsp olive oil
sea salt and freshly ground black
    pepper

For the herby spelt salad
120g (4¼oz) spelt
250ml (generous 1 cup) vegetable stock
    (bouillon)
1 tbsp olive oil
small handful of flat-leaf parsley,
    roughly chopped
small handful of mint leaves, roughly
    chopped
20g (¾oz) pistachios, chopped
35g (1¼oz) sultanas (golden raisins)

To serve
rocket (arugula)

Preheat the oven to 200°C (180°C fan)/400°F/gas 6.

For the herby spelt salad, add the spelt and vegetable stock (bouillon) to a pan, bring to the boil then reduce and simmer for 10 minutes until the spelt is tender.

While the spelt is cooking, prepare the fish parcels. Take two large pieces of parchment paper. Divide the fennel slices, arranging them in a pile in the middle of each piece of paper. Top each fennel pile with a halibut fillet, then lay over the slices of orange and sprinkle over the olives and parsley. Drizzle each piece with a generous glug of oil and season well with salt and pepper. Bring the sides of the parchment paper together to create a little tent, sealing well and tying with some kitchen string to ensure there are no gaps. Place the parcels onto a baking sheet and bake in the oven for 15–20 minutes.

Once the spelt is cooked, drain and place it in a large bowl. Mix together the olive oil, parsley, mint, pistachios, sultanas (golden raisins) and some generous seasoning.

Once the fish is cooked, remove from the oven and carefully open the parcels to reveal the beautiful, tender steamed fish. Serve alongside the spelt salad with some rocket (arugula).

Serves 2
–
Prep 15 mins
–
Cook 20 mins

Quick & Easy

CRISPY FRIED WHITEBAIT & WILD GARLIC TARTARE DIP

Whitebait are small white fish with very tender bones, which means you don't have to do any prep before frying and, once cooked, you can eat the fish whole. Fried as here, they make a delicious snack alongside an apéritif. As wild garlic is seasonal, you can easily substitute shop-bought garlic.

80g (2¾oz) plain (all-purpose) flour
1 tbsp smoked paprika
zest of 1 lemon, plus wedges to serve
vegetable oil, for frying
450g (1lb) whitebait
pinch of cayenne pepper
sea salt and freshly ground black
   pepper

For the wild garlic tartare dip

50g (1¾oz) wild garlic
100g (3½oz) natural (plain) yoghurt
50g (1¾oz) mayonnaise
1 tbsp capers, drained and rinsed
10 cornichons, finely diced
handful of dill, chopped

Make the wild garlic tartare dip: blitz the wild garlic with 25g (1oz) of the yoghurt in a food processor until it forms a smooth, green paste. Tip this into a bowl and mix with the remaining yoghurt, mayonnaise, capers, cornichons and dill. Season and set aside.

In a large bowl, mix together the flour, smoked paprika, lemon zest and some seasoning. Put the vegetable oil in a large, high-sided pan so that it comes at least 8cm (3in) up the sides. If you have a thermometer, heat the oil to 180°C (355°F). If you don't, test if the oil is hot enough by dropping in a small piece of bread or some breadcrumbs – you want it to sizzle and turn golden brown. Toss the whitebait in the seasoned flour and then fry them in the hot oil for 3 minutes until crispy and golden brown – you may need to do this in batches. Drain on paper towels.

When all the whitebait are fried, place them onto a platter and sprinkle over the cayenne pepper. Serve alongside the wild garlic tartare and some lemon wedges for squeezing.

Serves 4
–
Prep 10 mins
–
Cook 10 mins

PAN-FRIED MACKEREL WITH ROMESCO & ROASTED VEG

The combination of oily mackerel, romesco and butternut squash works brilliantly here for an easy yet impressive midweek meal. Romesco is a sauce traditionally made from tomatoes and originating from Catalonia; this version with roasted red peppers, nuts and chilli is spicy and flavoursome.

1 butternut squash, sliced into 2cm (¾in) half-moons
1 red onion, cut into wedges
1 tbsp olive oil, plus extra for drizzling
½ tsp fennel seeds
100g (3½oz) tenderstem or purple-sprouting broccoli
4 skin-on mackerel fillets
50g (1¾oz) cavolo nero (black kale), tough stalks removed and leaves shredded
50g (1¾oz) flaked almonds, toasted
sea salt and freshly ground black pepper

For the romesco
50g (1¾oz) blanched almonds, toasted
50g (1¾oz) walnuts, toasted
200g (7oz) jar roasted red (bell) peppers, drained
1 garlic clove, crushed
¼ tsp smoked paprika
¼ tsp chilli (red pepper) flakes
1 tsp sherry vinegar
4 tbsp extra virgin olive oil

Preheat the oven to 200°C (180°C fan)/400°F/gas 6.

Begin by making the romesco. Add the almonds and walnuts to a food processor along with the red (bell) peppers, garlic, smoked paprika, chilli (red pepper) flakes, sherry vinegar and olive oil. Blitz it together to form a rough paste. Taste and add seasoning, then set aside.

In a baking tin, add the butternut squash and red onion and drizzle with olive oil. Season well with salt and pepper and then scatter over the fennel seeds. Place in the middle of the oven and roast for 15 minutes. Add the broccoli and return to the oven for a further 10 minutes, until all the vegetables are tender.

While the vegetables are cooking, pan-fry the fish. Place a frying pan (skillet) over a medium heat and rub both sides of each fillet with olive oil and salt and pepper. When the pan is hot, add the fish, skin-side down, and fry for 3–4 minutes until the skin is really crispy, then flip and cook flesh-side down for a further minute. Remove the fish from the pan and add the shredded cavolo nero (black kale). Fry for 30 seconds before adding a splash of water and cooking until it has just wilted. Remove from the heat and add to the roasted vegetables.

To serve, add a bed of vegetables to each plate and top with a mackerel fillet. Spoon over some of the romesco and sprinkle on the toasted flaked almonds.

Serves 4
–
Prep 10 mins
–
Cook 30 mins

BAKED SMOKED HADDOCK WITH PUMPKIN & PANCETTA

Smoked haddock works really well with the earthy flavours of mushrooms, as well as pumpkin or squash and salty pancetta. This is a super-simple recipe which is all cooked in one dish and is packed full of flavour.

1 medium pumpkin or squash (such as sweet delica or crown prince)
4 banana shallots, cut into wedges
olive oil, for drizzling
250g (9oz) mixed wild mushrooms (such as oyster, enoki and chanterelle)
2 undyed, smoked, skinless haddock fillets
4 slices of pancetta
few sprigs of thyme
sea salt and freshly ground black pepper

Preheat the oven to 200°C (180°C fan)/400°F/gas 6.

Prepare the pumpkin or squash by slicing it into wedges or half-moons. Place these onto a large roasting tray along with the shallot wedges, drizzle with olive oil and season with salt and pepper. Roast for 20 minutes until the pumpkin or squash is beginning to soften.

After 20 minutes, add the mushrooms to the roasting tray. Place the fish fillets on top and place two pancetta slices onto each fillet. Drizzle with some more oil and sprinkle over the thyme. Return to the oven and roast for a further 10 minutes, until the fish is cooked through and the pancetta is crispy.

Remove from the oven and serve.

Serves 2
–
Prep 5 mins
–
Cook 30 mins

SMOKED HADDOCK RISOTTO WITH GREENS

Smoked haddock works beautifully in this creamy, soft risotto. Poaching the haddock first ensures it is cooked perfectly and is easy to flake and stir through. You can substitute the vegetables with any other greens you can get your hands on.

2 tbsp olive oil
1 onion, finely chopped
2 leeks, sliced
1.3 litres (5½ cups) vegetable stock (bouillon)
500g (1lb 2oz) smoked haddock
300g (10½oz) arborio risotto rice
250ml (generous 1 cup) white wine
100g (3½oz) frozen peas
100g (3½oz) frozen broad beans
1 courgette (zucchini), halved lengthways and then cut into 1cm (½in) slices
zest of 1 lemon
small handful of flat-leaf parsley, finely chopped
knob of butter
50g (1¾oz) Parmesan, finely grated, plus a little extra for the top
drizzle of extra virgin olive oil
sea salt and freshly ground black pepper

In a large pan over a medium heat, heat up some olive oil and add the onion and leeks with a pinch of salt. Fry gently for 5 minutes until they are really soft and turning translucent.

Meanwhile, pour the vegetable stock (bouillon) into a separate pan then add the smoked haddock fillets and leave them in the stock to poach for 5 minutes. When cooked through, remove the fish from the stock with a slotted spoon onto a plate. Discard the skin and flake the fish into chunks. Keep the stock pan warm over a low heat.

Once the onions and leeks have sautéed down, add the risotto rice and stir it through, making sure all the grains are well coated in the oil and vegetables. Allow the rice to fry gently for a minute or so. Then add the white wine and allow it to bubble away and the alcohol to evaporate. Once all the wine is absorbed, slowly add the hot stock, a ladleful at a time, stirring between each addition. Again, allow each addition of stock to be absorbed before adding the next. Keep doing this for 10 minutes (you may not need all the stock), until the rice tastes cooked but still has some bite.

Add the peas, broad beans and courgette (zucchini) to the risotto and allow them to cook for 5 minutes until the vegetables are cooked through. Add the flaked fish to the pan and stir through. Take the risotto off the heat and add the lemon zest, most of the parsley, the butter and the grated Parmesan. Stir this through to create a lovely, creamy risotto and add some seasoning.

Serve the risotto in bowls with some more grated Parmesan, the remaining parsley scattered on top and a drizzle of extra virgin olive oil.

Serves 4
–
Prep 10 mins
–
Cook 25 mins

CURRY-SPICED KEDGEREE WITH CAMARGUE RICE & RUNNY EGGS

Kedgeree is an Indian dish of spiced rice and often includes smoked fish, in this instance smoked haddock, and a soft-boiled egg. The warming curry spices make for a comforting and hearty meal – add some chilli oil for an extra-spicy kick.

120g (4¼oz) Camargue rice
450ml (2 cups) vegetable stock (bouillon)
1 tbsp coconut oil
1 onion, finely diced
2 curry leaves
1 tsp black mustard seeds
1 tsp cumin seeds
1 tsp fenugreek
1 tsp ground turmeric
1 tbsp mild curry powder
300g (10½oz) skin-on smoked haddock
300ml (10½fl oz) milk
2 eggs
100g (3½oz) frozen peas
juice of 1 lime
15g (½oz) coriander (cilantro), chopped

To serve
chilli oil (optional)

Add the rice to a pan and pour over the stock (bouillon). Bring to the boil and simmer gently for 20 minutes until the rice is nearly cooked, but there is still some liquid.

In a separate pan, heat the coconut oil, add the diced onion and fry until the onion is softened and translucent. Add the curry leaves, mustard seeds, cumin seeds, fenugreek, turmeric and curry powder. Let the spices fry for a minute or so until they are smelling toasty and fragrant. Add the rice to the pan and stir through.

Meanwhile, in a small pan, cover the smoked haddock with the milk, bring to the boil and then reduce to a gentle simmer. Cook for 5 minutes until the fish is just cooked through. Remove the fish with a slotted spoon onto a plate and pour the infused milk into the rice pan.

Remove the skin from the haddock and gently flake the fish.

Place a pan of water on to boil. Once boiling, reduce to a simmer and then gently lower the eggs into the water and boil for 7 minutes, before removing them from the pan and running under a cold tap to stop them cooking. When they are cool enough to handle, carefully peel them.

Add the frozen peas to the rice pan and cook for a minute before adding the lime juice and stirring through the flaked haddock. Slice the eggs in half.

Serve the kedgeree in bowls topped with the soft-boiled eggs. Scatter over the coriander (cilantro) and a drizzle of chilli oil, if desired.

Serves 2
–
Prep 15 mins
–
Cook 40 mins

THAI-STYLE SALMON PARCELS WITH GREENS & RICE

Steaming fish is not only a healthy way to cook it, it also ensures the fish stays moist. Wrapping this salmon up in parcels along with the greens and dressing means that each parcel is bursting with flavour and delicious cooking juices. It makes for a very quick and easy midweek meal.

120g (4¼oz) jasmine rice
100g (3½oz) choy sum, halved and
    sliced
3 baby pak choi (bok choy), halved
    lengthways
70g (2½oz) brown shimeji mushrooms
    (or shiitake if you can't find them)
2 skin-on salmon fillets
2 spring onions (scallions), thinly
    sliced, plus extra to garnish
1 red chilli, sliced into rounds
thumb-sized piece of ginger, peeled
    and cut into matchsticks
coriander (cilantro) leaves, to garnish

For the dressing
2 tbsp soy sauce
1 tsp runny honey
1 tsp sesame oil
2 garlic cloves, crushed
juice of 1 lime

To serve
1 lime, cut into wedges

Preheat the oven to 200°C (180°C fan)/400°F/gas 6.

Cook the jasmine rice according to the packet instructions.

Create your salmon parcels: using two large pieces of parchment paper, start by dividing and piling a base of the choy sum and pak choi (bok choy) between them. Then place the mushrooms on top of this and the fish on top of the mushrooms.

In a small bowl, whisk together the dressing ingredients. Drizzle this over the salmon fillets and then sprinkle over the spring onions (scallions), red chilli and ginger. Bring the sides of the parchment paper together to create a little tent, sealing well and tying with some kitchen string to ensure there are no gaps. Transfer to the middle of the oven for 15 minutes, until the fish is flaky and cooked through.

Carefully open the parcels to reveal the fragrant steamed fish and vegetables. Divide the rice between two plates and tip a parcel onto each one, ensuring you pour over all the delicious cooking juices. Garnish with some coriander (cilantro) leaves, sliced spring onions and some lime wedges on the side.

Serves 2
–
Prep 10 mins
–
Cook 15 mins

Quick & Easy

CRAB, CHILLI & TOMATO LINGUINE WITH PANGRATTATO

Crab linguine is a classic Italian dish prepared simply with chilli, tomatoes, white wine, parsley and lemon for a fresh flavour which lets the sweet crabmeat sing. *Pangrattato* means 'breadcrumbs' in Italian and is often referred to as the poor man's Parmesan; it's a perfect crunchy topping for pasta.

2 slices of slightly stale sourdough
2 garlic cloves, crushed
zest and juice of 1 lemon
4 tbsp olive oil
220g (7¾oz) dried linguine
150g (5½oz) baby cherry tomatoes, halved
½ red chilli, deseeded and finely diced
150g (5½oz) fresh white crabmeat
50ml (3 tbsp) white wine
small handful of flat-leaf parsley, chopped
sea salt and freshly ground black pepper

In a food processor, blitz up the sourdough slices until they are breadcrumbs. Tip them into a bowl and add one of the crushed garlic cloves, the lemon zest and 2 tablespoons of olive oil. Mix together well and then season with salt and pepper.

Heat up a frying pan (skillet) over a medium heat and tip in the oil-coated breadcrumbs. Fry them for 2–3 minutes until they turn golden brown and crispy. Tip out of the pan and into a bowl, setting aside for later.

Put a large pan of salted water on to boil. When it is boiling, add your linguine and cook according to the packet instructions, ensuring it maintains a little bite.

While the pasta is cooking, get a large frying pan over a medium heat and drizzle in 2 tablespoons of olive oil. Add the remaining crushed garlic clove, the cherry tomatoes and chilli to the hot oil and fry for 3 minutes, letting the garlic turn lightly golden and the tomatoes collapse and soften. Next add the crabmeat, letting it fry in the oils for a minute before adding the lemon juice and white wine. Allow the liquid to sizzle and cook down for an additional minute.

The pasta should be ready now. Use a mug to reserve a cup of the starchy pasta water, then use tongs to lift the cooked linguine out of its pan and straight into the crab pan. As soon as the pasta hits the pan, add a splash of the pasta water and toss it all together to make a silky sauce, coating everything evenly. Take the pan off the heat and add most of the parsley and some seasoning. If it is looking a little dry, then toss some more pasta water through it while it is still hot.

Serve the linguine in bowls topped with the lemon *pangrattato* and some additional chopped parsley sprinkled over the top.

Serves 2
–
Prep 10 mins
–
Cook 20 mins

CRAB GRATINS TOPPED WITH PARMESAN BREADCRUMBS

These rich, decadent gratins are a perfect starter for a dinner party (just scale up the ingredients as necessary) and feel like a real treat. The crème fraîche is a fantastic accompaniment to the creamy crab filling.

50g (1¾oz) butter
2 shallots, finely diced
4 garlic cloves, crushed
1 tsp smoked paprika
75ml (2½fl oz) white wine
150ml (5fl oz) vegetable stock (bouillon)
zest of 1 lemon, plus extra to garnish
300g (10½oz) mixed white and brown crabmeat
100g (3½oz) fresh breadcrumbs
25g (1oz) Parmesan, grated
1 tsp fennel seeds
pinch of chilli (red pepper) flakes
1 tbsp olive oil
2 tbsp crème fraîche
small handful of flat-leaf parsley, chopped
sea salt and freshly ground black pepper

Preheat the grill (broiler) to medium–high.

Melt the butter in a pan and add the shallots and a pinch of salt. Fry gently until the shallots have softened, then add the garlic and smoked paprika and cook for another couple of minutes. Next add the white wine, stock (bouillon) and lemon zest, and allow it to bubble before adding the crab and seasoning well. Take the mixture off the heat and decant into two small ovenproof ramekins.

Mix the breadcrumbs, Parmesan, fennel seeds, chilli (red pepper) flakes and olive oil in a small bowl. Season with black pepper and then top the ramekins with the mix.

Place the ramekins on a baking sheet under the grill for 5 minutes until golden and toasted on the top. Remove and add a dollop of crème fraîche, the chopped parsley and some lemon zest.

Serves 4
–
Prep 15 mins
–
Cook 10 mins

SEAFOOD & SWEETCORN CHOWDER WITH CROUTONS

This creamy and comforting chowder is absolutely delicious and a classic for good reason. Serve steaming bowlfuls of it topped with croutons and crispy lardons.

50g (1¾oz) butter
2 tbsp olive oil
2 celery sticks, finely diced
1 onion, finely diced
1 leek, finely diced
250g (9oz) floury potatoes, peeled and diced
1 tbsp plain (all-purpose) flour
1 bay leaf
150ml (5fl oz) white wine
600ml (21fl oz) fish stock (bouillon)
200ml (7fl oz) double (heavy) cream
2 slices of sourdough bread, cut into small chunks
150g (5½oz) smoked lardons
120g (4¼oz) sweetcorn
200g (7oz) firm, white skinless fish (such as cod, haddock or halibut), cut into chunks
170g (6oz) raw, peeled king prawns (jumbo shrimp)
8 scallops
small handful of flat-leaf parsley, leaves picked and chopped
sea salt and freshly ground black pepper

Preheat the oven to 200°C (180°C fan)/400°F/gas 6.

In a large pan set over a medium heat, add the butter and 1 tablespoon of olive oil. When hot, add the celery, onion, leek and potatoes and fry gently for 10 minutes until the vegetables have softened. Stir in the flour, allowing it to cook for 2 minutes, then add the bay leaf and white wine and let this bubble. Pour in the stock (bouillon) and cream and cook until the potatoes are tender.

In a large roasting tray, toss the sourdough chunks with 1 tablespoon of olive oil and season with salt and pepper. Toast them in the oven for 10 minutes until they are golden brown and crunchy.

In a small frying pan (skillet) fry the lardons until they are crispy.

When the potatoes are nearly done, add the sweetcorn, white fish, prawns (shrimp) and scallops. Allow them to cook for 5 minutes. Remove the bay leaf, add some seasoning and most of the chopped parsley.

Serve the chowder in bowls topped with the crispy lardons and croutons. Sprinkle over the remaining chopped parsley and enjoy.

YELLOW PRAWN LAKSA SOUP WITH NOODLES & GREENS

This soup uses a laksa paste for the base of its flavour, meaning it is incredibly simple to make. With creamy coconut, greens and fresh prawns (shrimp), it's a warming and fragrant midweek meal. Make sure to garnish with plenty of Thai basil and lime juice.

120g (4¼oz) folded flat rice noodles
3 tbsp laksa paste
1 tsp ground turmeric
400ml (14fl oz) tin coconut milk
300ml (10½fl oz) chicken stock
  (bouillon)
1 tbsp fish sauce
1 tbsp coconut cream
100g (3½oz) raw, shell-on king prawns
  (jumbo shrimp)
100g (3½oz) choy sum, leaves kept
  whole, stalks cut into 8cm (3in)
  pieces
50g (1¾oz) sugar snap peas, halved
  lengthways
100g (3½oz) beansprouts
2 spring onions (scallions), finely sliced
small handful of Thai basil leaves
1 lime, cut into wedges

Cook the noodles according to the packet instructions.

While the noodles are cooking, get a large pan over a medium heat and add the laksa paste and turmeric. Fry for 30 seconds before adding the coconut milk, stock (bouillon), fish sauce and coconut cream. Bring the soup to the boil before adding the prawns (shrimp), choy sum and sugar snap peas. Cook for approximately 2 minutes until the vegetables are tender and the prawns are cooked through.

Into deep bowls, add the flat noodles, then pour over the soup along with all the cooked vegetables and prawns. Top each bowl with some beansprouts, spring onions (scallions) and Thai basil leaves, and squeeze over some lime juice.

Serves 2
–
Prep 5 mins
–
Cook 15 mins

SARDINE & AUBERGINE PUTTANESCA WITH FETA

A simple and quick pasta dish using the versatile and humble tinned sardine. You can use any pasta shape you like, but a tubular one such as casarecce works well with the chunky sauce.

200g (7oz) casarecce pasta (or any other pasta)
2 tbsp olive oil, plus extra for drizzling
2 garlic cloves, sliced
½ tsp chilli (red pepper) flakes
1 small aubergine (eggplant), diced
95g (3¼oz) tin skinless, boneless sardines
400g (14oz) tin chopped tomatoes
50g (1¾oz) pitted black olives, halved
1 tbsp capers, drained and rinsed
handful of flat-leaf parsley, chopped, plus extra to garnish
50g (1¾oz) feta, crumbled
sea salt and freshly ground black pepper

Start by putting a large pan of salted water on to boil. When boiling, add the pasta and cook according to the packet instructions.

Meanwhile, make the sauce: in a large frying pan (skillet) over a medium heat, warm the olive oil, then add the garlic, chilli (red pepper) flakes and aubergine (eggplant). Fry for 3 minutes until the aubergine is softened and going golden brown. Next add the sardines and tomatoes and allow the sauce to bubble and heat through. Finally, add the black olives, capers and parsley, mix through and season.

Once the pasta is cooked, reserve a mug of the starchy cooking water. Use a slotted spoon to transfer the cooked pasta from the pan and into the sauce. Add a splash of the pasta water and toss the pasta in the sauce so it is well coated.

Serve the pasta in bowls and top with some crumbled feta, chopped parsley and a drizzle of olive oil.

Serves 2
–
Prep 5 mins
–
Cook 12 mins

Quick & Easy

SIMPLE SCALLOPS IN ZHOUG BUTTER

Zhoug is a spicy coriander- (cilantro-) based sauce originating from Yemen. This zhoug-flavoured butter is milder but has all the same flavours. Simply whip up the butter, spread over the scallops and pop under the grill (broiler) – it couldn't be simpler, but is such a tasty and flavoursome way to serve scallops.

1 tsp caraway seeds
½ tsp cumin seeds
small handful of coriander (cilantro), finely chopped
2 green chillies, deseeded and finely chopped
2 tbsp olive oil
2 garlic cloves, crushed
zest of ½ lemon
100g (3½oz) butter, softened
6 large scallops, cleaned and shells kept on

To serve
1 lemon, cut into wedges
sourdough

Begin by making the zhoug butter: in a small frying pan (skillet), toast the caraway and cumin seeds until they smell toasty and begin to pop. Remove from the pan and grind them with a pestle and mortar.

Add the ground spices to a food processor along with the coriander (cilantro), chillies, olive oil, garlic and lemon zest. Blitz to a paste. Tip the paste into a small bowl and mix in the softened butter.

Heat the grill (broiler) to medium–high. Place the scallops in their shells onto a baking sheet and add 1 heaped teaspoon of the zhoug butter onto each. Pop them under the grill for 5 minutes until slightly charred and the butter is melted and oozing.

Serve immediately with a squeeze of lemon and some bread to mop up the butter juices.

Serves 6
as a starter
–
Prep 10 mins
–
Cook 5 mins

GRILLED SQUID, CHICKPEAS, PEPPERS & CHERMOULA

Griddling squid for a very short time prevents it from becoming chewy and tough. The sweet, smoky chickpeas (garbanzo beans) work brilliantly with the zesty and herby chermoula sauce. Ask your fishmonger to prepare the squid, discarding the heads and gutting the bodies, leaving the tentacles.

2 tbsp olive oil
400g (14oz) tin chickpeas (garbanzo beans), drained and rinsed
3 roasted red (bell) peppers from a jar, drained and thinly sliced
1 tsp smoked paprika
1 tbsp tomato purée
100ml (3½fl oz) water
4 squid, heads discarded, body and tentacles gutted and kept whole
sea salt and freshly ground black pepper

For the chermoula
5 tbsp olive oil
3 garlic cloves, roughly chopped
25g (1oz) coriander (cilantro)
25g (1oz) flat-leaf parsley
juice of 1 lemon
2 tsp paprika
2 tsp ground cumin
pinch of cayenne pepper

To serve
1 lemon, cut into wedges

In a food processor, blitz together all the ingredients for the chermoula sauce. Check the seasoning and adjust to taste, then set aside.

In pan over a medium heat, heat up 1 tablespoon of olive oil. Add the chickpeas (garbanzo beans), roasted (bell) peppers, smoked paprika and tomato purée. Fry this for a minute until everything is smelling fragrant. Then add the water and allow the mixture to bubble and thicken for 2 minutes. Keep over a low temperature while you prepare the squid.

Cut the tentacles off the squid and slice the body into thick strips. Rub the squid with the remaining olive oil and season with salt and pepper. Heat up a griddle pan and, when hot, add the squid. Cook for 1–2 minutes on each side (if cooked for longer it can become very rubbery and tough).

Pile the smoky chickpea mixture onto a serving platter and top with the grilled squid. Drizzle over the chermoula sauce and serve with lemon wedges.

Serves 4
–
Prep 15 mins
–
Cook 15 mins

SOMETHING SPECIAL

These recipes are the feasts and the showstoppers – dishes to feed a crowd and to impress friends and family. They may take a little longer to prepare or have a few more stages, but they are worth the effort.

SEARED TUNA WITH SALSA VERDE & TOMATOES

This is an elegant and simple starter perfect for when you're entertaining. The delicious salsa verde pairs brilliantly with the oily, meaty tuna. It is worth spending a little more on good-quality tuna here, as it is prepared in such a pared-back way in order to allow the lovely ingredients to stand out.

400g (14oz) tuna steak
1 tbsp olive oil
200g (7oz) mixed-coloured cherry
   tomatoes, halved
sea salt and freshly ground black
   pepper
basil leaves, to garnish

For the salsa verde
20g (¾oz) flat-leaf parsley
10g (¼oz) basil
10g (¼oz) tarragon
1 tbsp capers, drained and rinsed
3 anchovy fillets
2 garlic cloves, crushed
2 tsp Dijon mustard
1 tbsp white wine vinegar
100ml (3½fl oz) extra virgin olive oil

Rub the tuna steak with a little olive oil and season on both sides with salt and pepper. Get a heavy-bottomed frying pan (skillet) over a medium–high heat. Once the pan is hot, sear the tuna for just 10 seconds on each side and then remove from the heat. Allow the tuna to cool a little, then place into the fridge until completely cold.

Next make the salsa verde: you can either blitz all the ingredients together in a food processor, bash them with a pestle and mortar or finely chop them by hand before mixing them well together. If you are using a food processor, pulse all the ingredients together until you have a bright green sauce (you can make this as smooth as you like, but it's nice to have a little texture still).

Thinly slice the chilled tuna into ½cm (¼in) pieces, cutting against the grain. Arrange the slices onto a serving platter. Scatter the cherry tomatoes on top of the fish, drizzle with the salsa verde and top with some basil leaves. Serve immediately – preferably al fresco and with some cold drinks to hand!

Serves 4
–
Prep 20 mins
plus chilling
–
Cook 5 mins

KERALAN MONKFISH CURRY WITH COCONUT RICE

This creamy and flavoursome South Indian-style curry uses monkfish, which has a distinctly meaty flavour and texture. It is perfect for absorbing the fragrant flavours from the curry. Double up the quantities to cook a feast for all your friends.

2 tbsp coconut oil
1 tsp mustard seeds
8 curry leaves
4 banana shallots, thinly sliced
3 garlic cloves, crushed
thumb-sized piece of ginger, peeled and grated
1 green chilli, finely chopped
2 tsp ground turmeric
1 tbsp tomato purée
splash of water
400ml (14fl oz) tin coconut milk
4 tomatoes, chopped
100g (3½oz) green beans
handful of spinach
500g (1lb 2oz) skinless monkfish, cut into chunks
sea salt and freshly ground black pepper

For the coconut rice
1 tbsp coconut oil
1 banana shallot, thinly sliced
150g (5½oz) long grain rice
100ml (3½fl oz) coconut milk
100ml (3½fl oz) vegetable stock (bouillon)

To serve
coriander (cilantro)
flatbreads (optional)
mango chutney (optional)

In a large, shallow pan, heat the coconut oil. Add the mustard seeds and curry leaves and allow them to sizzle and pop in the hot oil. Next add the shallots and gently fry for 5 minutes to soften before adding the garlic, ginger and chilli. Fry for another couple of minutes then add the turmeric and tomato purée with a splash of water, and allow it to bubble and create a paste. Tip in the coconut milk and tomatoes, bring to the boil and then reduce to a simmer for 10 minutes.

Make the coconut rice: in a pan over a medium heat, add the coconut oil and, once warm, add the shallot, frying until it has softened and is turning golden brown. Rinse the rice thoroughly in a sieve (strainer) under running water to remove any excess starch. Add the rice to the pan and stir it so it is well coated in the oil and shallot, frying for a minute or so. Tip in the coconut milk and vegetable stock (bouillon) and place a lid on the pan. Bring to the boil and then simmer for 10 minutes. Once the rice is cooked and has absorbed the liquid, take it off the heat, leaving the lid on to allow it to continue steaming.

After the curry has simmered for 10 minutes, add the green beans and spinach and cook for 1 minute. Add the monkfish and cook for 3–5 minutes (depending on how large the chunks are), until the fish is just cooked through and the beans are tender but still have some bite. Check the seasoning.

Remove the lid from the rice pan and fluff up the rice. Serve it alongside the monkfish curry, with some coriander (cilantro) sprinkled over and warm flatbreads and mango chutney, if you like.

Serves 4
–
Prep 20 mins
–
Cook 20 mins

Something Special

PANCETTA MONKFISH WITH PUY LENTILS & HISPI CABBAGE

Monkfish combined with pancetta, braised Puy lentils and buttery hispi cabbage makes for a very special dinner with minimal effort.

2 tbsp olive oil
1 small onion, finely diced
1 celery stick, finely diced
1 carrot, finely diced
2 garlic cloves, crushed
150g (5½oz) Puy lentils
2 sprigs of thyme, plus extra to garnish
1 bay leaf
370ml (13fl oz) vegetable stock
   (bouillon)
4 sage leaves
4 skinless monkfish fillets
8 slices of pancetta
1 tbsp olive oil
40g (1½oz) butter
1 large hispi cabbage, cut into
   4 wedges lengthways
sea salt and freshly ground black
   pepper

Preheat the grill (broiler) to medium–high.

In a large pan, heat the olive oil and add the onion, celery and carrot along with a pinch of salt. Fry gently for 5 minutes until the vegetables are beginning to soften. Add the garlic and fry for another couple of minutes. Then add the lentils, thyme and bay leaf and stir them around the pan, frying for another minute and making sure they are well coated in all the oil and vegetables. Pour in the stock (bouillon). Bring the mixture to a boil and then reduce to a simmer, cooking for 15–20 minutes until the lentils are just tender but still have a little bite. Season with salt and pepper.

While the lentils are cooking, prepare the monkfish. Place one sage leaf on each monkfish fillet and then wrap each with two slices of pancetta. Place the wrapped fillets onto a baking sheet and drizzle with some olive oil and cracked black pepper. Place under the grill for 5–10 minutes, until the fish is cooked through and the pancetta is lovely and crispy.

Prepare the hispi cabbage: place a large frying pan (skillet) over a medium heat and add the butter. Once it has melted and is foaming, add the cabbage wedges cut-side down. Allow them to cook for a few minutes on each side so they char and turn lovely and golden. Turn the cabbage in the pan so it cooks evenly on all sides. Remove from the pan and season well with salt and pepper.

Place the monkfish fillets on a bed of the steaming, aromatic lentils. Add a wedge of buttery hispi cabbage on the side and sprinkle over some thyme sprigs.

Serves 4
–
Prep 10 mins
–
Cook 30 mins

MONKFISH & PRAWN SKEWERS WITH YOGHURT

These skewers are made extra special with marinated monkfish and prawns (shrimp). They make wonderful barbecue alternatives to the usual fare, and are great for feeding a crowd with all the extra accompaniments.

3 tbsp olive oil
small handful of mint, chopped, plus leaves to garnish
1 tsp za'atar
1 tbsp red wine vinegar
juice of ½ lemon
450g (1lb) skinless monkfish, cut into chunks
2 red (bell) peppers, deseeded and cut into chunks
2 onions, cut into wedges
300g (10½oz) raw, peeled tiger prawns (shrimp)
4 flatbreads
50g (1¾oz) rocket (arugula)
100g (3½oz) pomegranate seeds
drizzle of pomegranate molasses (optional)
sea salt and freshly ground black pepper

For the quick-pickled onions
100ml (3½fl oz) cider vinegar
1 tbsp caster (superfine) sugar
1 tsp salt
1 red onion, finely sliced

For the sumac yoghurt
100g (3½oz) natural (plain) yoghurt
1 tsp sumac
1 lemon, zested

You will also need 8 wooden or metal skewers. If you are using wooden skewers, soak them in water for 30 minutes before using.

Start by making the quick-pickled onions. In a bowl, add the vinegar, sugar and salt and whisk together until the sugar and salt have dissolved. Add the red onion, mix and set aside while you continue with the recipe.

In a large bowl, mix together 2 tablespoons of olive oil, mint, za'atar, red wine vinegar and lemon juice. Season well and add the monkfish, (bell) peppers, onions and prawns (shrimp), mixing well. Let the fish and vegetables marinate for 30 minutes while you prepare the other elements.

In a small bowl, mix together the yoghurt, sumac, lemon zest and some seasoning. Set aside.

After the fish and vegetables have marinated, carefully thread the pieces onto your skewers, alternating between monkfish, peppers, onions and prawns.

Heat up your barbecue or alternatively your griddle pan. Once hot, cook your skewers for approximately 3 minutes on each side, turning them so they cook evenly – you want the vegetables and fish to char and soften. Once the skewers are cooked, pop the flatbreads on to warm up on each side for 1 minute. Toss the rocket (arugula) in 1 tablespoon of olive oil.

Now you are ready to serve. Remove the tender, chargrilled fish and vegetables from the skewers and pile onto flatbreads. Spoon over some sumac yoghurt and add some rocket leaves, pickled red onions, pomegranate seeds, mint leaves and a drizzle of pomegranate molasses, if using. Fold up the flatbreads and enjoy!

Serves 4
–
Prep 20 mins
plus marinating
–
Cook 10 mins

Something Special

SWEET & SMOKY SEAFOOD TAGINE WITH COUSCOUS

This smoky, tomatoey tagine is packed full of white fish and seafood, making it a really special dinner to cook for friends. Served with couscous, minted yoghurt and flatbreads, the whole spread is great for larger numbers.

2 tbsp olive oil
2 onions, thinly sliced
3 garlic cloves, crushed
1 tsp ground cumin
1 tsp ground coriander
1 tsp smoked paprika
1 tsp ras el hanout
1 tbsp tomato purée
500ml (2 cups) fish stock (bouillon)
100g (3½oz) cherry tomatoes
70g (2½oz) pitted green olives, halved
500g (1lb 2oz) white fish, cut into
    chunks (cod, halibut or haddock
    work well)
150g (5½oz) squid rings and tentacles
200g (7oz) raw, peeled prawns
    (shrimp)
large handful of coriander (cilantro),
    roughly chopped, plus extra to
    garnish
sea salt and freshly ground black
    pepper

For the couscous
200g (7oz) couscous
2 tbsp olive oil
200ml (7fl oz) vegetable stock
    (bouillon)

For the mint yoghurt
150g (5½oz) natural (plain) yoghurt
handful of mint, chopped, plus extra
    to garnish
1 tbsp olive oil

To serve
warm flatbreads
crunchy green salad

Heat the oil in a large, heavy-bottomed casserole dish placed over a medium heat. Once the oil is hot, add the onions with a pinch of salt and fry for 5 minutes until softened. Next add the garlic and fry for another minute before adding the spices. Fry for another minute until the spices are smelling fragrant. Next add the tomato purée, fish stock (bouillon), cherry tomatoes and green olives. Bring this to the boil and simmer for 30 minutes until the sauce has thickened.

While the sauce is cooking, prepare your couscous by placing it in a large bowl and pouring over the olive oil and some seasoning. Pour the hot vegetable stock over the couscous. Without stirring, pop a clean dish towel over the bowl and allow the couscous to steep and cook for 10 minutes.

In a small bowl, mix together the yoghurt, mint, olive oil and some seasoning. Set aside.

Returning to the tagine, now you can add the fish, squid and prawns (shrimp) for 3 minutes until they are cooked through. Take off the heat and sprinkle over the coriander (cilantro). Check the couscous – it should be lovely and tender when you use a fork to fluff it up.

Serve the tagine alongside the couscous, minted yoghurt and warmed flatbreads. Garnish with some coriander and mint leaves. This dish goes beautifully with a crisp and crunchy fresh salad to contrast with the smoky tagine.

Serves 4
–
Prep 15 mins
–
Cook 45 mins

SPANISH-STYLE STUFFED SQUID BAKED IN TOMATO SAUCE

These stuffed squid are so delicious, with a rich tomato sauce and tasty rice filling. They are an exceptionally good dinner party choice. Ask your fishmonger to prepare the squid for you.

2 tbsp olive oil
1 onion, finely diced
4 garlic cloves, crushed
50g (1¾oz) chorizo, finely diced
½ tsp fennel seeds
50g (1¾oz) pitted green olives, finely chopped
1 tsp capers, drained and rinsed
1 tbsp tomato purée
15g (½oz) flat-leaf parsley, finely chopped, plus extra to garnish
120g (4¼oz) basmati rice
300ml (10½fl oz) vegetable stock (bouillon)
4 medium squid
sea salt and freshly ground black pepper

For the tomato sauce
1 tbsp olive oil
2 garlic cloves, crushed
100ml (3½fl oz) dry sherry
680g (1lb 8oz) passata

To serve
crusty bread

Preheat the oven to 200°C (180°C fan)/400°F/gas 6.

Heat 2 tablespoons of olive oil in a pan, add the onion and a pinch of salt and fry gently for about 5 minutes until softened and translucent. Next add the garlic and fry again for a minute or so before adding the chorizo and fennel seeds. Fry for 2–3 minutes until the chorizo has crisped up. Add the olives, capers, tomato purée, parsley, basmati rice and vegetable stock (bouillon). Bring to the boil and then reduce to a simmer for 12–15 minutes until the rice is tender but still has a little bite. Season well.

In a separate pan, make the sauce: heat up the olive oil over a medium heat. When hot, add the garlic and fry for a minute until it turns lightly golden. Next add the sherry followed by the passata. Allow the mixture to bubble and thicken slightly for 5 minutes. Season the sauce well with salt and pepper.

Take each squid and rinse under water. Carefully stuff the cavity with the rice mixture. Arrange them in a row in a baking dish, pour over the sauce and bake for 20 minutes.

Serve the stuffed squid with some chopped parsley sprinkled on top and some warm crusty bread alongside.

Serves 4
–
Prep 20 mins
–
Cook 50 mins

SEAFOOD ORZO PAELLA WITH SAFFRON & HERBS

Paella is perfect for a crowd and looks wonderful with its vibrant colours and seafood. This version uses orzo instead of traditional paella rice, which is a small pasta that soaks up all the tomato sauce and juices. If using clams here, soak them for 20 minutes in cold water before adding them to the orzo.

2 tbsp olive oil
1 onion, diced
2 garlic cloves, crushed
60g (2¼oz) chorizo, diced
3 tbsp tomato purée
250ml (generous 1 cup) white wine
pinch of saffron
½ tsp smoked paprika
500ml (2 cups) chicken stock (bouillon)
350g (12oz) orzo
200g (7oz) either mussels or clams (or a mixture), scrubbed and debearded
12 shell-on prawns (shrimp)
180g (6¼oz) squid, cut into rings and tentacles kept whole
½ lemon, juiced
15g (½oz) flat-leaf parsley and dill, chopped

In a large, wide, lidded frying pan (skillet) set over a medium heat, pour in the olive oil. Once the oil is hot, add the onion and a pinch of salt and fry off for 5 minutes until it is soft and translucent. Add the garlic and chorizo and fry for a further 2 minutes until the chorizo starts to crisp up.

Next add the tomato purée and stir it through, followed by the wine, saffron, smoked paprika and chicken stock (bouillon). Bring the liquid up to the boil and then add the orzo. Let the orzo cook for 6 minutes, until nearly cooked, then add the mussels or clams. Place the lid on the pan and let them steam for 3 minutes. After this time, they should be open, and the insides cooked (discard any that have not opened). Now add the prawns (shrimp) and squid and let them bubble in the paella for 1–2 minutes.

Squeeze over the lemon juice and garnish with the fresh herbs. Bring the whole, impressive-looking pan to the table and serve up.

Serves 6
–
Prep 5 mins
–
Cook 25 mins

CIDER-STEAMED CLAMS WITH SMOKED HAM

Clams are sweet and delicate in flavour. When paired with dry (hard) cider and smoky ham, these are utterly moreish – just make sure to have some warm, crusty bread on hand to soak up all the delicious juices!

40g (1½oz) butter
1 onion, finely diced
3 garlic cloves, finely chopped
200g (7oz) smoked gammon (ham) or smoked bacon, finely diced
450ml (2 cups) dry (hard) cider
1 tbsp wholegrain mustard
1kg (2lb 4oz) clams, soaked in cold water for 20 minutes
15g (½oz) flat-leaf parsley, finely chopped
few slices of sourdough bread, griddled or toasted
sea salt and freshly ground black pepper

In a large pan with a tight-fitting lid, warm the butter over a medium heat. Once the butter has melted and is foaming, add the onion and a pinch of salt. Fry for 5 minutes until it has softened and is turning translucent, then add the garlic and continue to fry for a further minute.

Next add the smoked ham or bacon, and fry for 3–4 minutes until starting to crisp up. Once you have lovely crispy bits in the pan, add the cider and wholegrain mustard. Bring to the boil and then reduce the temperature before tipping in the clams and popping the lid on.

Allow the clams to cook and steam in the liquid for 3–4 minutes, shaking the pan to encourage them to open up. After 4 minutes the clams should be opened up and the insides cooked through (discard any that haven't opened). Take the lid off and sprinkle over the parsley.

Serve the clams and their sauce in bowls, with toasted bread on the side to soak up the delicious juices. Bring another bowl to the table to collect the shells.

> Serves 2
> –
> Prep 5 mins
> plus soaking
> –
> Cook 15 mins

Something Special

SPAGHETTI VONGOLE WITH SPICY NDUJA SAUCE

Vongole is a classic Italian pasta dish made with clams. This version uses nduja, a soft, spicy sausage meat from Calabria in southern Italy, which melts into a beautiful sauce when fried.

200g (7oz) spaghetti or linguine
2 tbsp olive oil
2 garlic cloves, sliced
50g (1¾oz) nduja sausage
100g (3½oz) cherry tomatoes, finely diced
75ml (2½fl oz) white wine
500g (1lb 2oz) clams, soaked in cold water for 20 minutes
50g (1¾oz) cavolo nero (black kale), shredded
handful of flat-leaf parsley, finely chopped
sea salt and freshly ground black pepper

Place a large pan of salted water on to boil. When boiling, add the pasta and cook according to the packet instructions – it should be al dente, retaining a little bite.

While the pasta is cooking, heat up the olive oil in a large frying pan (skillet) with a fitted lid. When hot, add the garlic and fry for 30 seconds before adding the nduja sausage and tomatoes. Cook this for 3 minutes, breaking up the nduja with the back of a spoon so it melts and creates a sauce.

After 3 minutes, add the white wine, clams and cavolo nero (black kale) and put the lid on the pan. Allow the clams to cook and steam for 3 minutes, shaking the pan occasionally to encourage them to open. After 3 minutes they should be open and cooked through (discard any that remain shut).

Once the pasta is cooked, reserve a mug of the starchy cooking water. Use tongs to lift the pasta from the water and straight into the clam pan. Add a splash of the starchy water and then toss well to ensure that all the pasta is well coated in the sauce. Season well with salt and pepper and sprinkle through the chopped parsley.

Serves 2
–
Prep 5 mins
plus soaking
–
Cook 15 mins

SALMON & PRAWN LASAGNE WITH ASPARAGUS

This lasagne is utterly delicious and will be popular with the whole family! The combination of the greens and pesto make it lighter than the classic lasagne made with bolognese, and the fish and prawns (shrimp) are kept moist when cooked through the sauce.

50g (1¾oz) butter
1 leek, finely chopped
50g (1¾oz) plain (all-purpose) flour
550ml (2¼ cups) milk
80g (2¾oz) fresh pesto
100g (3½oz) baby spinach, roughly
    chopped
300g (10½oz) skinless salmon fillets,
    cut into cubes
250g (9oz) raw prawns (shrimp),
    roughly chopped
150g (5½oz) fine asparagus spears,
    roughly chopped
8–12 lasagne sheets
25g (1oz) Parmesan, finely grated
sea salt and freshly ground black
    pepper

Preheat the oven to 220°C (200°C fan)/425°F/gas 7.

Start by making the roux: melt the butter in a saucepan and, once foaming, add the leeks and cook gently for 5 minutes until softened but not catching. Add the flour and stir so the leeks are well coated, then continue to cook the flour for a couple of minutes. Slowly add the milk, a splash at a time, beating it in after each addition. Keep going until all the milk is added and you have a creamy sauce, add some seasoning and then allow it to cook for 2 minutes to thicken up.

Next add the pesto and spinach and stir through until the spinach has wilted. Scatter a third of the salmon, prawns (shrimp) and asparagus into the bottom of a baking dish, then pour over a third of the pesto roux sauce. Top this with a layer of lasagne sheets (you may need to cut some of the sheets to fit the dish). Repeat these steps twice more before finishing with a layer of the lasagne and some of the roux sauce. Sprinkle over the grated Parmesan.

Bake for 30–35 minutes until golden brown on top.

Serves 4–6
–
Prep 10 mins
–
Cook 1 hour

HARISSA SIDE OF SALMON WITH BULGUR & CARROTS

This dish is designed to feed a group, using a beautiful roasted side of salmon. However, if you are wanting to cook for fewer people you can easily halve the recipe and use salmon fillets instead – just make sure to reduce the cooking time to 10 minutes.

200g (7oz) baby rainbow carrots
2 tbsp olive oil
1 tsp cumin seeds
1 side of skin-on salmon (about 850g/1lb 14oz)
2 tbsp harissa paste
1 lemon, sliced
100g (3½oz) feta
1 tbsp dukkha
sea salt and freshly ground black pepper

For the bulgur salad
250g (9oz) bulgur wheat
500ml (2 cups) vegetable stock (bouillon)
15g (½oz) flat-leaf parsley, finely chopped
15g (½oz) mint, finely chopped, plus extra to garnish
40g (1½oz) pomegranate seeds
zest and juice of 1 lemon

Preheat the oven to 200°C (180°C fan)/400°F/gas 6.

Into a large baking tin lined with baking paper, add the baby carrots and drizzle with 1 tbsp of olive oil, the cumin seeds and some seasoning. Toss them so they are well coated and then spread them out around the edges of the tin. In the middle of the tin place the side of salmon, skin-side down. Spread the harissa paste onto the flesh and rub across evenly. Top the fish with some lemon slices, drizzle with the remaining oil and add some seasoning. Place into the middle of the oven for approximately 20 minutes, until the fish is just cooked through and the carrots feel tender.

While the salmon and carrots are roasting, prepare the bulgur salad. Place the bulgur and stock (bouillon) in a large pan and bring to the boil, then reduce to a simmer and place the lid on the pan. Cook the bulgur for 15 minutes until the liquid is absorbed and the grains are tender. Remove from the heat and leave with the lid on for 10 minutes to steam, then fluff it through with a fork. Transfer to a large bowl and mix through the herbs, lemon zest and juice and 30g (1oz) of the pomegranate seeds. Season well and set to one side.

When you are ready to serve, lay a bed of the bulgur salad at the bottom of a large serving platter. Scatter the roasted carrots on top and crumble over the feta. Place the beautiful side of salmon on top and sprinkle with the dukkha, remaining pomegranate seeds and some mint leaves. Bring to the table and serve everyone from the big feasting platter.

Serves 6
–
Prep 10 mins
–
Cook 25 mins

Something Special

SALMON, COURGETTE & BROCCOLI TART

Using ready-made puff pastry means this is a super-simple and stress-free way to create an impressive-looking tart. The lemony mascarpone is delicious alongside the salmon, courgette (zucchini) and broccoli. Don't skip the griddling of the courgette though – the charring looks lovely and adds flavour.

1 courgette (zucchini), thinly sliced lengthways
2 tbsp olive oil, plus extra for drizzling
50g (1¾oz) tenderstem broccoli tips
1 × 320g (11¼oz) puff pastry sheet
250g (9oz) mascarpone
zest of 1 lemon
small handful of chives, finely chopped
2 small, skinless salmon fillets, cut into 2½cm (1in) strips
1 egg, beaten
10g (¼oz) chives, chopped very finely, plus extra to garnish
sea salt and freshly ground black pepper

To serve
green salad

Preheat the oven to 200°C (180°C fan)/400°F/gas 6.

Heat up a griddle pan and brush the courgette (zucchini) strips on each side with olive oil. Once the pan is hot, cook the strips in batches for 2 minutes on each side so they get char lines. Once they are cooked on both sides, remove from the pan and set aside.

While you are cooking the courgette strips, place a pan of water on to boil. When boiling, drop in the broccoli tips and blanch for 30 seconds before draining and running under cold water to stop them cooking further.

Unroll the puff pastry sheet and place it on a large baking sheet lined with baking paper. Use a knife to score out a border all around, roughly 2cm (¾in) wide. In a small bowl, mix together the mascarpone, lemon zest, chives and plenty of seasoning. Spread the mascarpone mixture evenly up to the border.

Dot the salmon strips on top of the mascarpone. Do the same with the blanched broccoli and then finish with the courgette strips. Drizzle with olive oil and brush the beaten egg carefully around the border.

Place the tart into the oven for 20 minutes until the fish is cooked and the pastry is puffed up and golden.

Remove from the oven and scatter over some more chives. Slice into portions and serve alongside salad for a deliciously fancy lunch.

Serves 6
–
Prep 10 mins
–
Cook 30 mins

COCONUT, TURMERIC & LEMONGRASS MUSSELS

Nothing beats a big bowl of fragrant, steaming mussels. This recipe uses a coconut-milk base for the sauce and is flavoured with turmeric and lemongrass. Serve on the table, with a bowl for the empty shells and spoons to make sure you scoop up all the flavoured sauce.

1 tbsp coconut oil

2 shallots, finely sliced

2cm (¾in) piece of ginger, peeled and grated

2 garlic cloves, grated

1 lemongrass stalk, tough outer leaves discarded, finely chopped

1 red chilli, deseeded and finely chopped

1 tsp ground turmeric

1 tsp galangal paste

400ml (14fl oz) tin coconut milk

1 tsp fish sauce

1kg (2lb 4oz) mussels, scrubbed and debearded

handful of coriander (cilantro) leaves, to garnish

1 lime, cut into wedges

In a large pan with a tight-fitting lid, heat the coconut oil over a medium heat. When the oil has melted, add the shallots and fry gently for 5 minutes until softened. Next add the ginger, garlic, lemongrass and chilli and fry for a further 2 minutes. Once these have softened too, add the turmeric and galangal paste and fry for a minute, making sure everything is well coated. Pour in the coconut milk and fish sauce and bring up to the boil. Add the mussels and pop the lid on the pan. Allow the mussels to steam in the sauce for 5 minutes, occasionally giving the pan a shake to encourage the shells to open.

After 5 minutes, the mussels should be open and cooked – discard any that have remained shut.

Serve the mussels in big, steaming bowls, ladling over the remaining sauce (and bring an extra bowl to the table for all your empty shells). Garnish with the coriander (cilantro) leaves and squeeze over some lime.

Serves 2
–
Prep 10 mins
–
Cook 15 mins

Something Special

FISH TACOS WITH CHIPOTLE YOGHURT & SALSA

Fish tacos are a fantastically fun sharing meal. These are wonderfully simple but with all the sides and toppings it feels like a feast. Bring all the elements to the table and let everyone dig in and assemble their own. Great when served with refreshing lime margaritas for a real Mexican fiesta!

4 skin-on white fish fillets (such as cod or haddock)
100ml (3½fl oz) olive oil, plus a little extra for frying
2 tbsp apple cider vinegar
juice of 1 orange
½ red cabbage, finely shredded
200g (7oz) natural (plain) yoghurt
1 tsp chipotle paste
1 avocado, sliced
juice of 2 limes
16 small corn tortillas (I like the brand Cool Chile)
15g (½oz) coriander (cilantro), leaves picked
sea salt and freshly ground black pepper

For the marinade
50ml (3 tbsp) olive oil
zest and juice of 1 lime
1 tsp ground cumin
1 tsp smoked paprika
¼ tsp cayenne pepper
½ tsp garlic granules

For the salsa
2 corn on the cobs
a little olive oil
½ mango, chopped
2 vine tomatoes, diced
½ red chilli, deseeded and finely chopped
zest and juice of 1 lime
small bunch of coriander (cilantro), chopped

In a large bowl, mix the marinade ingredients with plenty of seasoning. Add the fish fillets and coat well. Place the bowl in the fridge and marinate for 15 minutes.

For the salsa, place a griddle pan on a medium–high heat. Lightly brush both corn cobs with a bit of olive oil. Once the pan has heated up, cook the corn on all sides, allowing the kernels to char a little. Remove from the heat and allow to cool. In a small bowl, mix together the other salsa ingredients. Once the corn has cooled, stand each cob upright and use a knife to shave off the corn kernels. Add the kernels to the remaining salsa. Mix well and season.

In a large bowl, mix together the apple cider vinegar and orange juice. Add the cabbage and a good pinch of salt and gently scrunch the cabbage into the dressing and set aside. This will lightly pickle and soften the cabbage.

Mix the yoghurt with the chipotle paste, season with salt and set aside. Squeeze the juice of 1 lime over the sliced avocado.

In a large frying pan (skillet), heat up a splash of olive oil. Once the pan is hot, fry the marinated fish, starting skin-side down, for roughly 2–3 minutes to allow the skin to get crispy and golden brown. Meanwhile get a small pan over a medium–high heat. When hot, add the tortillas and dry-cook for a minute on each side. Keep them warm by wrapping in a clean dish towel while you heat the rest. Once the fish skin is crispy, flip the fillets over and cook for about a minute until the fish is cooked through. Set aside on a plate.

Bring all the elements to the table for everyone to help themselves: warm tortillas, flaked fish, salsa, pickled cabbage, avocado, chipotle yoghurt, coriander (cilantro) leaves and a squeeze of lime.

Serves 4
–
Prep 40 mins plus marinating
–
Cook 5 mins

EASY FISH PIE WITH CELERIAC, POTATO & CARROT MASH

Fish pie is a classic and a firm family favourite. This recipe is packed full of white fish, salmon and prawns (shrimp). The root vegetable topping is a tasty take on traditional potato mash.

100g (3½oz) butter
1 onion, sliced
2 leeks, sliced
50g (1¾oz) plain (all-purpose) flour
200ml (7fl oz) white wine
100ml (3½fl oz) double (heavy) cream
1 tsp wholegrain mustard
15g (½oz) flat-leaf parsley, chopped
100g (3½oz) frozen peas
150g (5½oz) firm, white skinless fish (haddock, cod, pollock or coley all work well), cut into chunks
150g (5½oz) skinless salmon, cut into chunks
300g (10½oz) skinless smoked haddock, cut into chunks
150g (5½oz) raw, peeled prawns (shrimp)
300g (10½oz) celeriac (celery root), peeled and roughly chopped
400g (14oz) floury potatoes, such as Maris Pipers, peeled and roughly chopped
200g (7oz) carrots, peeled and roughly chopped
50ml (3 tbsp) milk
50g (1¾oz) butter
sea salt and freshly ground black pepper

To serve
green veg

Preheat the oven to 200°C (180°C fan)/400°F/gas 6.

In a large pan, heat up the butter. When it is melted and foaming, add the onion and leeks and gently fry until they are soft and translucent.

Stir in the flour so the vegetables are well coated, cooking for a minute or so until it starts to smell biscuity. Gradually pour in the wine, a splash at a time, mixing in after each addition. After you have added all the wine you should have a creamy sauce. Let it simmer for 3–5 minutes until thickened and the alcohol has cooked off. Take the sauce off the heat and stir through the cream, mustard, parsley, peas, all the fish and the prawns (shrimp). Transfer the fish pie base into a heatproof pie dish or high-sided baking tin and set to one side.

Place the celeriac (celery root) and potatoes in a large pan and fill with cold water and a pinch of salt. Bring the water up to the boil and then reduce to a simmer. Cook for 10 minutes and then add the carrot and cook for a further 10 minutes, until everything is tender and cooked through. Drain the vegetables and mash or put through a ricer until smooth. Add the milk and the butter and mix through. Season well with salt and pepper.

Spoon the root vegetable mash on top of the fish pie base and level it out evenly. Use a fork to create lines down the mash (this helps create crunchy bits when baking).

Place in the middle of the oven and bake for 30–40 minutes until it is golden brown on top and bubbling hot in the middle. Serve alongside some piled-up greens.

Serves 6
–
Prep 15 mins
–
Cook 1 hour

PAN-FRIED SCALLOPS WITH CAULIFLOWER & CHORIZO

Pan-fried scallops and cauliflower, two ways, are a great combination in this delicious, restaurant-worthy dish.

1 large cauliflower, chopped into florets
1 red onion, cut into wedges
60g (2¼oz) chorizo, diced
1 tbsp capers, drained and rinsed
drizzle of olive oil
50g (1¾oz) butter
100ml (3½fl oz) milk
100ml (3½fl oz) single (light) cream
a little nutmeg, grated
6 scallops
25g (1oz) hazelnuts, toasted and
    roughly chopped
sea salt and freshly ground black
    pepper
few flat-leaf parsley leaves, to garnish

For the vinaigrette
3 tbsp olive oil
1 tbsp balsamic vinegar
juice of ½ lemon
1 tsp runny honey

Preheat the oven to 200°C (180°C fan)/400°F/gas 6.

Divide the cauliflower florets in half, keeping one half back for the purée. Put the other half into a roasting tin along with the red onion wedges, chorizo and capers. Drizzle with olive oil and season with salt and pepper, then roast in the middle of the oven for 20–25 minutes.

Meanwhile, make the cauliflower purée. Place the remaining cauliflower florets in a pan with half of the butter and gently cook for 3 minutes until beginning to turn lightly golden. Tip in the milk and cream and cook for a further 2 minutes until the cauliflower is tender. Grate in a little nutmeg and season with salt and pepper before tipping the whole mixture into a blender or food processor and blitzing until smooth.

In a medium frying pan (skillet) over a medium–high heat, add the remaining half of butter. When the butter has melted and is foaming, fry the scallops on each side for approximately 2 minutes, basting them as they cook to create a lovely golden edge. Remove from the pan and season well.

To serve, spoon some cauliflower purée on the bottom of the plate and then pile on the roasted cauliflower, onion, chorizo and capers. Once the roasting tin is empty, use the remaining chorizo oil in the pan to create your vinaigrette – simply whisk the vinaigrette ingredients into the hot tin.

Top the plates with the pan-fried scallops, spoon over some warm vinaigrette and scatter over the hazelnuts and parsley.

Serves 2
–
Prep 15 mins
–
Cook 30 mins

WHOLE SALT-BAKED SEA BASS

Salt-baking is a wonderful technique and, despite appearances, it doesn't make it overly salty. Instead, it flavours it perfectly and the salt crust allows the fish to steam within its own juices, so you are left with tender, soft flesh. Simply served with buttery new potatoes and greens, the sea bass really shines.

1 whole sea bass (about 600g/1lb 5oz), gutted and descaled (or you can use snapper, salmon or trout)
handful of parsley
handful of dill
4 sprigs of thyme
1 lemon, sliced

For the salt crust
500g (1lb 2oz) rock salt
100g (3½oz) dill, finely chopped
3 egg whites

To serve
new potatoes
green salad

Preheat the oven to 220°C (200°C fan)/425°F/gas 7. Line a large baking tin with baking paper.

Stuff the cavity of the fish with the fresh herbs and lemon slices, placing some of the lemon slices on the top of the fish, too.

In a large bowl, mix together the salt, dill and the egg whites, combining until it resembles wet sand. Place some of the salt mixture onto the bottom of the lined baking tin and spread it out. Place your stuffed sea bass onto the salt and then, using the remaining salt mixture, encase the fish, leaving just the head and tail exposed.

Place the fish into the oven and bake for 25 minutes (for a larger fish, give it 40 minutes). Remove it from the oven and use a wooden spoon or rolling pin to carefully crack the salt crust, then remove it in pieces to reveal the tender fish. Fillet the sea bass and serve alongside buttery steamed potatoes and fresh salad.

Serves 2
–
Prep 15 mins
–
Cook 25 mins

Something Special

ROAST SEA BASS WITH POTATOES, FENNEL & TOMATOES

Roasting and serving a whole fish is a special thing and looks impressive at the table – and it's incredibly easy to prepare. As the sea bass bakes, all the juices flavour and combine with the base of potatoes and fennel. For extra ease, ask your fishmonger to prepare the sea bass for you.

1 sea bass, gutted
1 onion, sliced
5 garlic cloves
1 fennel bulb, cut into wedges
1kg (2lb 4oz) waxy potatoes, thinly sliced
2 tbsp olive oil
juice of 1 lemon
2 bay leaves
4 sprigs of thyme
1 tsp caraway seeds
1 tsp cumin seeds
1 lemon, sliced
4 sprigs of rosemary
300g (10½oz) cherry tomatoes on the vine
small handful of flat-leaf parsley, roughly chopped

Preheat the oven to 200°C (180°C fan)/400°F/gas 6.

In a large roasting tray, add the sliced onion, garlic cloves, fennel wedges and sliced potatoes. Drizzle this with the oil and lemon juice and then scatter over the bay leaves and half the thyme. Season well, cover with foil and place into the preheated oven for 30–35 minutes.

After 30–35 minutes, remove the tray from the oven and take off the foil. Sprinkle over the caraway seeds and cumin seeds. Slash the fish five times on each side and then stuff the cavity with the rosemary, the remaining thyme, and some of the lemon slices. Place the fish on top of the potatoes and add any remaining lemon slices on top. Then place it back into the oven for a further 30 minutes.

When the fish has been cooking for 15 minutes, remove it from the oven and add the vine tomatoes around the fish. Place the whole tray back into the oven for the remaining 15 minutes.

Remove the tray from the oven and sprinkle over the chopped parsley. Bring the whole tray to the table and let everyone serve themselves.

Serves 4
–
Prep 10 mins
–
Cook 1.5 hours

SARDINE FISH BALLS IN CREAMY MUSTARD SAUCE

These succulent fish balls are flavoured with herbs, raisins and pine nuts. Served alongside a creamy, mustardy sauce it feels like a special meal. You can bulk it out by adding rice or quinoa with the sauce poured over and some greens alongside.

140g (5oz) tin skinless, boneless sardines
2 shallots, finely diced
20g (¾oz) raisins
25g (1oz) pine nuts, toasted
2 eggs, beaten
100g (3½oz) fresh breadcrumbs
small handful of parsley, finely chopped, plus extra to garnish
small handful of dill, finely chopped
zest of 1 lemon
2 tbsp olive oil
sea salt and freshly ground black pepper

For the creamy mustard sauce
1 tbsp olive oil
1 shallot, finely sliced
150ml (5fl oz) white wine
200ml (7fl oz) double (heavy) cream
1 tbsp wholegrain mustard
1 tbsp flat-leaf parsley, chopped

To serve
wild rice or quinoa
wilted greens

Drain the sardines from the oil and add them to a large bowl, mashing them with a fork to break them up. Add the shallots, raisins, pine nuts, beaten eggs, breadcrumbs, herbs and lemon zest. Season well and then mix to combine. Roll the mixture out into 18–20 equal-sized balls.

In a large frying pan (skillet) heat up the olive oil over a medium heat. Fry the fish balls for 8–10 minutes until golden on all sides.

In another pan, make the creamy mustard sauce: heat the olive oil and add the sliced shallot with a pinch of salt. Fry this gently for 5 minutes before adding the white wine. Let this sizzle and then add the cream, wholegrain mustard and parsley. Season well.

Once the fish balls are cooked, transfer them to the creamy mustard sauce and stir though. Serve alongside some wild rice or quinoa and wilted greens. Garnish with a little cracked black pepper and some parsley leaves.

Serves 4
–
Prep 15 mins
–
Cook 15 mins

Something Special

VIETNAMESE-STYLE CRAB CAKES WITH PAPAYA SALAD

These flavour-packed crab cakes are completely irresistible, especially paired with the punchy, fresh papaya salad. If you can't get hold of green papaya, you can use kohlrabi, carrot or beansprouts instead.

200g (7oz) white crabmeat
1 red chilli, deseeded and finely diced
5cm (2in) piece of ginger, peeled and grated
15g (½oz) coriander (cilantro), finely chopped
2 spring onions (scallions), finely chopped
2 tbsp soy sauce
1 egg, beaten
100g (3½oz) fresh breadcrumbs
2 tbsp neutral oil (such as vegetable oil)

For the papaya salad
juice of 2 limes
2 tsp soft brown sugar
1 tsp fish sauce
1 green papaya, cut into matchsticks
1 carrot, cut into matchsticks
50g (1¾oz) mangetout (snow peas), thinly sliced lengthways
½ red onion, thinly sliced
small handful of coriander (cilantro), chopped
small handful of Thai basil, chopped, plus extra to garnish
20g (¾oz) salted peanuts, chopped

To serve
sweet chilli dipping sauce

In a large bowl, mix together the crab, chilli, ginger, coriander (cilantro), spring onions (scallions) and soy sauce. Mix so that everything is evenly distributed. Next add the beaten egg and breadcrumbs, and mix again. Shape the mixture into eight equal-sized patties and pop them into the fridge while you mix the papaya salad.

Prepare the papaya salad: in a large bowl, whisk together the lime juice, sugar and fish sauce until the sugar dissolves. Then pile in the papaya, carrot, mangetout (snow peas), red onion and herbs and toss it well so that everything is evenly coated. Sprinkle over the chopped peanuts and some extra Thai basil leaves.

Heat a large frying pan (skillet) over a medium–high heat and pour in the oil. Fry the crab cakes for 3 minutes on each side until golden brown (you may need to fry in batches depending on the size of your pan). Remove from the pan and place onto some paper towels to absorb any excess oil.

Serve the crab cakes with the papaya salad and some sweet chilli dipping sauce on the side.

Serves 2–4
–
Prep 30 mins
–
Cook 10 mins

CRAB, GRUYÈRE, SPRING ONION & HERB QUICHE

This is a truly decadent and special quiche. The delicate and sweet flavours of the crab marry beautifully with the gruyère and herbs. This makes a lovely centrepiece for a lunch or buffet, but alternatively you could make smaller, individual-sized ones as a delicious starter.

flour, for dusting
320g (11¼oz) shortcrust pastry
2 egg yolks
3 eggs, beaten
150ml (5fl oz) double (heavy) cream
200g (7oz) white crabmeat
100g (3½oz) brown crabmeat
100g (3½oz) gruyère, finely grated
4 spring onions (scallions), finely sliced
1 tbsp chives, finely chopped
1 tbsp tarragon, finely chopped
sea salt and freshly ground black
     pepper

To serve
dressed salad

Preheat the oven to 200°C (180°C fan)/400°F/gas 6.

On a lightly floured surface, roll out the pastry so it is more than large enough to fit a 20cm (8in) deep, fluted tin. Lay the pastry over the tin and then press it into the base and sides. Leave the edges hanging over the sides of the tin and gently press fork marks into the base. Pop the tin into the fridge for 10 minutes.

After 10 minutes, scrunch up some baking paper, open it up again and lay it onto the pastry. Fill with baking beans and then put the tin onto a baking sheet. Transfer to the middle shelf of the oven and blind bake for 15 minutes. After 15 minutes, remove the paper and baking beans and then return to the oven for a further 5 minutes – you want the pastry to be very lightly golden and to feel chalky to the touch. Remove from the oven (but keep the oven on) and brush the bottom and sides of the pastry with one of the beaten egg yolks, then use a sharp knife to carefully trim the pastry edges. Set aside.

In a large jug or bowl, mix together the three eggs with the remaining yolk and the cream. Add the crabmeat, cheese, spring onions (scallions) and herbs. Season the whole mixture generously.

Return the baking sheet, with the pastry tart case on top, to the middle shelf of the oven. Carefully pour in the egg mixture as far up to the top as possible, being cautious not to spill the filling. Bake for 30–35 minutes until there is a slight wobble still in the middle. Remove from the oven and allow to cool slightly before slicing. Serve with crisp, dressed salad.

Serves 4-6
–
Prep 20 mins
plus chilling
–
Cook 1 hour

ROAST SEA BREAM WITH FATTOUSH-STYLE SALAD

Fattoush is an Arabic salad made from toasted, crispy bread, tomatoes and cucumber. Flavoured with sumac, it's light, tasty and packed with flavour, and works perfectly alongside roasted sea bream. Cooking the whole fish is a wonderful way to ensure the fish is tender and makes for a special dinner.

1 whole sea bream, gutted and descaled
1 lemon, sliced
2 tbsp olive oil
1 tsp sumac
small handful of flat-leaf parsley, roughly chopped
sea salt and freshly ground black pepper

For the dressing
juice of ½ lemon
1 tsp sumac
1 garlic glove, minced
1 tsp pomegranate molasses (optional)
1 tbsp olive oil
1 tsp red wine vinegar

For the fattoush-style salad
2 pitta breads
2 tbsp olive oil
½ red onion, finely sliced
2 baby cucumbers, halved lengthways, deseeded and then sliced into half-moons
100g (3½oz) cherry tomatoes, halved
1 romaine lettuce, shredded
4 radishes, finely sliced
handful of mint, leaves picked
handful of flat-leaf parsley, leaves picked
80g (2¾oz) pomegranate seeds

Preheat the oven to 200°C (180°C fan)/400°F/gas 6.

Place the sea bream in a baking tin lined with baking paper and slice diagonal lines into the flesh on both sides of the fish. Place some of the lemon slices in the cavity and the rest on top. Drizzle the whole fish with olive oil, sprinkle over the sumac and then season well with salt and pepper, rubbing it well into the fish. Scatter over the parsley and place into the oven to roast for 20 minutes.

While the fish is cooking, prepare the fattoush-style salad. In a small bowl, whisk together all the ingredients for the dressing.

Toast the pittas until they are golden brown and then break them up into roughly bite-sized pieces. Add the pitta pieces into a large bowl and drizzle over some oil and season with salt and pepper. In another large bowl, mix together the red onion, cucumber, tomato, lettuce, radishes and herbs. Pour the dressing into the bowl and toss it all together so everything is well coated. Add the toasted pitta pieces and scatter over the pomegranate seeds.

Serve the fattoush salad alongside the roasted sea bream.

Serves 2
–
Prep 15 mins
–
Cook 20 mins

INDEX

ACKNOWLEDGEMENTS

It is always daunting when you embark on a big project – with 60 recipes to write and a book to fill with images, this felt like a mammoth task, but it has been an utter joy to work on and I am so pleased with the final product. There are a few very special people whose help and guidance have been fundamental to the making of this book.

I would like to start by thanking my family and friends, who have always supported every new project I take on and are my biggest cheerleaders – their love and support have been constant and so greatly appreciated.

Thank you to Octavia, who took on a chunk of my recipes to test and gave such concise notes and feedback (and positive messages about how delicious her favourites were!).

Thank you to my editor Stacey, who despite not being able to be on set or to chat through things in person, has always been on the end of the phone or email (or WhatsApp!) to guide me through this project and always reassure me that things were looking good. We have worked on a fair few projects together now, and I hope we can continue to do so. Thank you to Alicia for her equal support and guidance – nothing is too much to ask of Alicia and her constant sunny disposition was so welcome.

The creative team behind the shooting of a cookbook is always collaborative and incredibly inspiring. Thank you to Louie for your beautiful props – you have such a good eye and always choose the most unique and lovely pieces. Rita, the talented photographer behind the images in this book – thank you for bringing my recipes to life. We had such fun on the shoot, so many laughs, and thankfully had very similar visions for each shot (often resulting in finishing each other's sentences). Also, you (and your boyfriend's) encouraging and positive feedback on the recipes was exactly what I needed! Thank you to Sarah and Sophie for your incredible assistance – we had a big shot-list to get through each day and you were both so reliable, upbeat and supportive throughout. I couldn't have done it without you.